Dedication

In gratitude to all

the small-congregation

pastors and laity

who shared their stories.

This work is yours.

And the kingdom is

already among you.

Endorsements

Teresa Stewart has faith in the future of small congregations because she has faith in a God who shows up even in small and forgotten places. She believes that small churches are neither deficient nor immature but rather critical learning laboratories as the church navigates a future far too complex for one-size-fits-all patterns of ministry. *The Small Church Advantage* offers a hopeful vision and practical resources for vital small church worship that is indigenous and incarnational, hands-on, not hierarchical, participatory rather than performative. It is a poignant reminder that the future God beckons us toward is more like a handful of tiny mustard seeds than a grove of stately sequoia trees.

F. Douglas Powe, Jr.
Director of Lewis Center for Church Leadership, Wesley Theological Seminary

Whereas the Roman Empire was all about grandeur and greatness, Jesus preached about tiny seeds, about having a small amount of faith. 'Bigger is better' isn't just the motto of our culture but, in too many instances, our churches too, especially when it comes to Sunday morning worship. In this remarkable, small book, Stewart demonstrates that smaller churches aren't inferior; they have an advantage. Plant these ideas in the soil of your congregation and see what happens!

Mike Graves
William K. McElvaney Professor Emeritus of Preaching and Worship, Saint Paul School of Theology

Teresa Stewart's passion for and commitment to small congregations is evident on every page of this book. More importantly, she turns the conversation about small congregations away from a focus on their perceived deficiencies and disadvantages and toward their giftedness and advantages. Then, by redirecting conversations about worship away from a focus on performance and toward collaboration and participation, she helps us identify how attention to a congregation's giftedness can reshape its experience of worship and the connections it makes between worship and daily life. The result is an accessible, creative, and practical resource for the thousands of small congregations across the church.

E. Byron (Ron) Anderson
Styberg Professor of Worship, Garrett-Evangelical Theological Seminary

The Small Church Advantage belongs in the hands of both clergy and laity. Stewart has refined an easy-to-read, rhythmic writing style that turns serious worship talk into lively kitchen-table conversation. Like the Early Church and our 16th-century reformers, she builds on the idea of worshipers as active participants: worship is the work of ALL the people, not just a small group of expert leaders. The examples, explanations (and humor!) will fill you with hope and a spirit of adventure. Imagine—2,000 years later, and we're just getting started!

Susan Marie Smith

Episcopal Priest, Retired Professor of Worship, Scholar of Lay Ministry

The Small Church Advantage is the best book on the small church I have ever read. It is not only the subtlety of Stewart's mind or the clarity of her writing; it is the relentless creativity concretely applied to worship in the small church. Working with the difference between the performance aesthetic of the large church and the participation aesthetic of the small church, she has wonderful ideas and quite practical examples that can revolutionize worship in the small congregation.

Tex Sample

Robert B. And Kathleen Rogers Professor Emeritus, Saint Paul School of Theology

Finally, a book for small churches from someone who understands and appreciates small churches! Teresa Stewart names the oft-overlooked beauty and gifts of small membership churches while providing a practical, theologically rich framework to rediscover and renew their worship. Small churches have something important to teach the wider Church about worship, and Stewart's book will help them do just that.

Allen Stanton

Former Director of the Turner Center for Rural Vitality
Author of *Reclaiming Rural: Building Thriving Rural Congregations*

Teresa's work has transformed the way we do worship. We're no longer trying to imitate big places. We've found our own gifts to offer God! During the week, I run into people who are already talking about what might happen this week. In the past year, participation has gone through the roof. And Sundays have started feeling like the best kind of potluck celebration.

Rebecca Stredney

Pastor, Great Plains Conference of The United Methodist Church

The
Small Church
Advantage

Seven Powerful Worship Practices
that Work Best in Small Settings

Teresa J. Stewart

Market
Square
BOOKS

The Small Church Advantage

Seven Powerful Worship Practices that Work Best in Small Settings

©2023 Teresa J. Stewart

books@marketsquarebooks.com
141 N. Martinwood, Suite 2 Knoxville, Tennessee 37923

ISBN: 978-1-950899-72-2

Printed and Bound in the United States of America
Cover Illustration & Book Design ©2023 Market Square Publishing, LLC

Editor: Sheri Carder Hood
Post-Process Editor: Ken Rochelle
Page Design: Carrie Rood
Cover Design: Kevin Slimp

Scripture quotations used with permission from:

CEB

Scripture quotations from the COMMON ENGLISH BIBLE. © Copyright 2011 COMMON
ENGLISH BIBLE. All rights reserved. Used by permission. (www.CommonEnglishBible.com).

NRSV

New Revised Standard Version Bible, copyright © 1989 National Council
of the Churches of Christ in the United States of America.
Used by permission. All rights reserved worldwide.

NIV

Scriptures marked NIV are taken from the NEW INTERNATIONAL VERSION (NIV):
Scripture taken from THE HOLY BIBLE, NEW INTERNATIONAL VERSION ®. Copyright©
1973, 1978, 1984, 2011 by Biblica, Inc.™. Used by permission of Zondervan.

MES

THE MESSAGE: THE BIBLE IN CONTEMPORARY ENGLISH (MES):
Scripture taken from THE MESSAGE: THE BIBLE IN CONTEMPORARY ENGLISH,
copyright©1993, 1994, 1995, 1996, 2000, 2001, 2002. Used by
permission of NavPress Publishing Group

Contents

Introduction

The Small Congregation Advantage
Seven Lessons for a Whole-Church Conversation

There are painful flaws in our conversations about small congregation worship. Dressed up, they sound like this:

Small congregations don't really have what is needed for quality worship. At best, they fumble through it. Their music doesn't measure up. The preaching is weak. It's not entirely their fault (bless their hearts). They struggle without adequate expertise, or vision, or resources to consistently pull off powerful worship.

Oh, yes, and we are exhausted at the endless task of trying to fill in the holes for them.

But what if I told you that small congregations have powerful advantages in offering worship—deeply forming strengths that are not generally available in big settings?

They do.

And what if our current approach to small congregations largely strips these powerful strengths and replaces them with putty and paint to better imitate worship in large congregations?

It does.

So, would it be worth some messy exploration—*a*

1

conversation—if there were another way?

I fervently believe it is. For small congregations. And for the work of the whole Church. *Bless our hearts.*

PART 1

DEAR CHURCH, CAN WE TALK?

Seven Lessons for a Whole-Church Conversation

Lesson 1: Small Congregation Worship Matters

> For everyone.
>
> And not just for now.
>
> *Really.*

Lesson 2: Just the Facts

> There are loads of small congregations.
>
> And they work differently from big ones.

Lesson 3: Saying the Quiet Part Out Loud

> We value big congregations—*a lot.*
>
> So we've made them the measuring stick for excellent worship.
>
> With some troubling consequences.

3

Lesson 4: The Monkey Wrench of Incarnation

Replacing the measuring stick.

With mess, vernacular, difference.

And good news.

Lesson 5: In Search of a Small-Congregation Toolbox

New clues from an old source—*aesthetics.*

The different rules of big-setting performance.

And small-setting participation.

Lesson 6: Training up Artisans

Experimenting, flailing, innovating . . .

And learning to work with small congregation tools.

Again.

Lesson 7: The Participation Advantage

A practical and theological case:

Curating worship with the strengths of small congregations.

For the whole Church.

Chapter One

Lesson 1: Small Congregation Worship Matters
Seven Lessons for a Whole-Church Conversation

For everyone.

And not just for now.

Really.

Dear Church,

Let's start with this fundamental agreement about worship. It's a truth Christians share whether we describe our worship as contemporary, traditional, hybrid, or house. It's our common commitment, even without a common denomination or affiliation. It holds up regardless of whether we order worship in two, four, or six parts. And it's true whether we worship alongside twelve or twenty thousand.

Curious?

Here it is. And, fair warning, it's scandalous. God—the author of life, beyond all space, time, and reason—comes to be with us. In worship, God joins us. Just as we are. Right where we are. Wherever we are. Christian worship isn't simply a messaging opportunity for the gathered. Or a who-does-it-best performance. Or some kind of think-about-this event. Christian worship is nothing less than a divine-human encounter. An actual meet-up between God and God's people. *God present*—for a local, mutual exchange of communication and gifts. *God present*—to grow a gracious, unimaginable relationship between the High Holy and the Right Here.

Jesus promised, "I am with you" whenever two or three are gathered in his name (Matthew 18:19-20). But this promise was not some new divine initiative. Scripture is thick with the indiscriminate intimacy of divine love. God shows up in glorious temples. But God also chases after us in dusty traveling tents. God meets us in the rubble of what used to be a glorious temple. But also joins us at ordinary dinner tables. And in stale underground tombs. Divine love demonstrates a wildly reckless disregard for ideal settings and perfect people.

All of this means that small-congregation worship matters. Not once it improves the music and preaching. Or when it better imitates the practices of big congregations. Or when the attendance numbers make it worth God's RSVP. Small-congregation worship matters for this simple, essential, primary, theological reason: God shows up.

But there's more. Small-congregation worship doesn't simply matter to small-congregation worshipers. It matters to *all* worshipers.

The salvation story can't be told without an enormous range of divine show-up stories. Scripture even insists that God has a peculiar preference for doing new things in small settings, unexpected places, and with unlikely people.

God shows up in crowded city centers. But also on lonely wilderness roads. God shows up for big gatherings like the 5,000 folks fed with miraculous bread, fish, and hope. But also for small disruptions—like the woman pouring out pricey perfume for a priceless truth.

God shows up for large faithful bunches. But also for scoundrels like Jacob, disrupters like Ruth, wafflers like Nicodemus, and uppity outsiders like the Canaanite woman.

Apparently, we need all these divine encounters to see how far God is willing to go to be with us. We need small, unexpected, and unlikely encounters to grasp the fullness of the good news. Or perhaps so it can grasp us.

There's still more. Small congregations also matter to the *future* of the whole Church—in all places.

Really?

Small congregations are crucial local laboratories. They are places of indigenous experimentation. Small congregations are diagnostic centers tasked with figuring out what the good news sounds like and looks like in each community. To help grow the kingdom in the years ahead.

The late Phyllis Tickle helps explain. She reminds us that there are predictable, roughly 500-year cycles in our faith tradition.[1] Within each 500-year cycle, new experiments emerge at the margins and edges alongside older, established practices at the center.

Around the end of each 500-year cycle, there's a major transition. We collectively—and irritably—sort out what to keep (because it's working and faithful) and what to get rid of (because it's not). This sorting results in a kind

---

[1] Phyllis Tickle, *The Great Emergence: How Christianity is Changing and Why* (Ada, MI: Baker Books, 2008), based on the idea and metaphor of Ralph Adams Cram in *The Great Thousand Years*, 1910.

of chaotic Church "rummage sale" of structures and practices. And, not surprisingly, it's marked by immense change and heightened anxiety.

Sound familiar?

But the results of this irritable sorting process are also reassuring, according to Tickle. Because somehow, after each transition, the Church doesn't collapse, shrink, and die. Somehow ministries expand. New things are unleashed. Outrageously, some of the small, unexpected, unlikely experiments work. And from these experiments, we end up with more local models. More indigenous innovations. For more people. In more places. And with a greater diversity of forms and practices.

God shows up.

But there may be a new wrinkle in the ancient pattern that Tickle describes. Currently, we are abundantly confident in the successes of our large congregations. And our confidence may be changing the rules of this rummage sale. Especially in the United States. We may be preserving and replicating general worship models that work in well-resourced, large settings. And overlooking everything else—like the messy, unpredictable particulars of small settings.

We are not exploring how large and small congregations might work differently, then teaching the strengths of each. Instead, we are looking for successful, one-size-fits-most answers with a troubling result: we are gathering all the kingdom's eggs into one big basket. And missing the margins and edges where local ministries might be incubating unnoticed.

Please note. This is not a plea to save all small

congregations. Human organizations have life cycles. Not all can or should be saved. There are unhealthy congregations of *all* sizes.

Instead, this is a call:

- To unleash small congregations—*differently.*
- To see God present in the workings of small congregations—*differently.*
- To reimagine worship through small congregations' distinctive communities—*differently.*
- To make small congregations (again) local laboratories, indigenous innovators, and good news diagnosticians.

Answering this call won't be easy. It will take us to unexpected, unsettled, untidy edges (as it always has). It will require experimenting, flailing, and learning. And we will have to learn how to do this work *with* and not simply *for* small congregations. So we don't return to merely replicating one model.

The historical pattern is pretty clear. Some small congregations and unlikely ministries will resource the Church through the next great transition.

Ultimately, returning to the practices of local laboratories should feel familiar to the Church. It's rooted deeply in our tradition and incarnational theology. It also resonates with God's outrageous preference for doing new things with scoundrels, wafflers, and uppity outsiders (*bless all of our hearts*).

Really.

Let's talk.

Chapter Two

Lesson 2: Just the facts

Seven Lessons for a Whole-Church Conversation

There are loads of small congregations.

And they work differently from big ones.

Plenty of groups are genuinely concerned with small congregations. These groups reach across all denominations in all fifty states. Each group is filled with faithful, ministry-loving, kingdom-seeking folks. And each group shares a sense that something isn't working.

But that's where the commonalities end. Perspectives differ.

Denominational leaders worry that their small congregations simply aren't flourishing. Many are dying: *They need so many fixes. It's hard to know where to start.*

Small-congregation pastors and laity feel overwhelmed, misunderstood, and dismissed: *We need something different. Big-congregation resources don't fit. Training events meant to inspire us leave us feeling more shame than hope.*

Seminary professors are troubled that new pastors are isolated in small congregations at the very time they need the most support: *Small-setting appointments are less like a call to ministry and more like a requirement to pay their dues. Mostly on their own. Then move to something bigger.*

Talented, innovative leaders in big congregations are often puzzled. They pour their very best gifts into developing excellent resources. And they graciously pass them along to small congregations: *We know these practices work well. Of course, it's up to the small congregations to adapt them, maybe dial them down. But at least it's a start, right?*

But is it the right start? What do small congregations *need?*

There are lots of perspectives and few genuine conversations among these groups. So maybe it's time we start with two well-studied, straightforward facts that all of these faithful groups can agree on.

1. **The vast majority of congregations in the U.S. are small.**
   There are around 177,000 small congregations—churches with fewer than 95 weekly worshipers.[2] It's the reality across denominations and across rural, urban, and suburban settings. While 70 percent of worshipers attend a congregation with an attendance of 250 or more, 70 percent of all congregations are, in fact, small. And a majority of these include fewer than 65 weekly worshipers.

---

[2] Hartford Institute for Religion Research: http://hartssem.edu/research/fastfacts. See also National Congregation Study of 2018: https://sites.duke.edu/ncsweb/files/2022/02/NCSIV_Report_Web_FINAL2.pdf

2. Small congregations are not big places in miniature.

Small congregations differ dramatically from big ones in a variety of ways—like demographic pull, organizing systems, community stresses, financial and other resources, staffing, and pastoral responsibilities.

These differences make comparing big and small congregations a little like comparing cats and apples. A few real-world details highlight some challenges in treating them like the same thing.

- Worshipers with less education and income are more likely to attend a small congregation. So, there are class issues quietly tucked alongside size issues.

- Big congregations (or even medium-sized ones) are not an option for many rural areas, transient communities, and new immigrant groups.

- The largest proportion of small-congregation budgets typically goes to repairing and maintaining an older, often less-than-ideal building.

- Small congregation pastors may be volunteer, bi-vocational, or serve two or three congregations at a time. Their job descriptions require them to be jacks-of-all-trades and staffs-of-one. They may provide pastoral care for communities in different counties. They may drive 50 miles or more among congregations each Sunday. They oversee budgets, complete a growing stack of denominational paperwork, worry about boilers, plan weekly worship, prepare sermons, troubleshoot technology, and frequently type their own bulletins.

- While large congregations make new investments in affluent, up-and-coming areas, small ones more frequently find themselves in economically stagnant areas. With many neighbors in need.

- The number of small congregations is growing.

These may not be the facts we would like. But God's used to that. Divine love takes on real-world messes and makes do. It can launch a rescue plan for creation with a ragtag bunch of former slaves, an uncredentialed fisher with poor impulse control, and a scandalously pregnant teenager.

So God probably doesn't shy away from these facts.

Neither should we.

Chapter Three

Lesson 3: Saying the Quiet Part Out Loud
Seven Lessons for a Whole-Church Conversation

We value big congregations—*a lot.*

So we've made them the measuring stick for excellent worship.

With some troubling consequences.

This is an anxious time for the Church in the United States. The fear of decline pokes at us. Over the last twenty years, average worship attendance has dropped by half. In 2000, the median size of congregational worship was 137. Now it's 65.[3]

So it's not surprising that the successes of large congregations have been reassuring for us. Their numbers offer a fear-of-decline antidote. And we've rightfully cherished their work. After all, they've led innovations in contemporary worship and liturgical renewal. They've launched movements that have swept across the United States and reshaped Protestant worship![4]

---

[3] https//research.lifeway.com/2021/10/20/small-churches-continue-growing-but-in-number-not-size.

[4] Lester Ruth and Lim Swee Hong, *A History of Contemporary Praise & Worship: Understanding the Ideas that Reshaped the Protestant Church* (Ada, MI: Baker Academic, 2021).

15

Large congregation practices have been inspirational, important, and powerful.

But they've also become—well, *limiting*.

This is the quiet part we need to say out loud: big congregations have become the goal. They are no longer one worship model among many. They are seen as the ideal. The measuring stick against which other worship should be compared.

And this quiet part is more than a hunch. Drs. Lester Ruth and Lim Swee Hong offer insight in *A History of Contemporary Praise and Worship: Understanding the Ideas that Reshaped the Protestant Church*. Their work documents the rise of two muscular "rivers" that have carved out the current landscape of worship. First, there's the "River of Praise and Worship," which seeks to meet up with God through lavish expressions of praise. And second, there's the "River of Contemporary Worship," which seeks relevant worship updated for contemporary people.

Both rivers are big movements that include faithful folks seeking the kingdom of God. Together these muscular movements have innovated and reimagined how we think about worship. But they have also silently nudged small congregations out of the innovating and imagining.

How?

The "Praise and Worship" model is resource intensive. Praise bands require a swirl of experts, equipment, facilities, and rehearsal—not the resources of an average-sized gathering of 65 people. The "Contemporary Worship" model is rooted in growth expectations and marketing science. So success is measured primarily by increased attendance. Other messy markers of vitality suited to small congregations are overlooked[5] as if evaluating the health of cats and apples requires a single checklist.

And there are more troubling consequences to this quiet part. With big-congregation measuring sticks clenched firmly in one hand, it's been a short step from *different* to *inferior* for small congregations.

You can hear it in the well-intentioned language of calling small congregations "not-yet-big" ones. The phrase is meant as encouragement. But the point is clear: small congregations aren't what they *should* be.

You can hear it in the consulting wisdom of The Effective Church Group, which represents three decades of work with more than a thousand congregations across a variety of denominations. The appeal is blunt.[6] A central article on its website explains "Why Large Churches Are More Effective than Small Churches." The language of *size* is conflated with "success," "influence," "excellence," and "effectiveness." This logic paints small congregations as stunted, failure-to-thrive places. The site urges readers to retweet "Every large church was once a small church," with the implication that *thank God they got over it, and maybe you can, too.*

---

[5]   Allen T. Stanton, *Reclaiming Rural: Building Thriving Rural Congregations* (Lanham, MD: Rowman & Littlefield, 2021). Stanton reminds us that the population in rural communities "will not typically sustain numeric growth." Further, many other types of vitality markers are skewed toward medium and large congregation practices, 27-29.

[6]   http://effectivechurch.com.

Small is treated as either defective or immature.

Another troubling consequence of this treatment is its multiplication effect. The Church seems to have planted a one-way sign between small and large congregations with a confidence that carries the whiff of toxic charity.[7] Worship resources, expertise, and value flow solely in one direction. From large to small. Never the other way around. The Effective Church Group candidly claims that small congregations' "brand of ministry is possible only with the support of larger churches."

Not surprisingly, large congregations do not see themselves as potential beneficiaries of distinctive small-congregation gifts. Because—another quiet part—we are not really sure that small congregations have any. This one-way sign sets the Church up for the next troubling consequence: a cycle of pathologizing. We've treated small congregations as more "holey" than holy. Then started filling in the holes.

The problem with this kind of cycle is recognized across disciplines. It's cautioned against in everything from architecture to family systems, start-up companies, and institutions of educations. The analysis goes like this. In imagining better buildings, relationships, organizations or learning, it matters where you start. Starting with the *strengths* (what's working) gets you to a different design than starting with the *weaknesses* (what's broken).

A strength-based approach unleashes new possibilities: *Hey, what could we build with these?*

---

7   See Robert D. Lupton, *Toxic Charity: How Churches and Charities Hurt Those They Try to Help* (San Francisco: HarperOne, 2011) and Steve Corbett's and Brian Fikkert's, When Helping Hurts (Chicago: Moody Publishers, 2012). Apart from emergencies, one-way signs between givers and receivers are actually red flags.

A weakness-based approach preserves an ideal. Then makes a list of fix-it projects for all the places where the actual doesn't measure up to the ideal.

Sound familiar? It's the approach we've applied to small congregations. We have focused on the small-setting holes (or pathologies) in the context of that one right, big-setting worship model. Then we've gotten stuck in an endless loop: *Find hole. Putty. Paint. Repeat. Repeat. Repeat. Repeat.*

Strengths or weaknesses, we tend to find what we look for, and unfortunately, we've been looking for weaknesses in small congregations. We've measured their impediments to replicating big-congregation successes. We've sought fixes to music, preaching, and technology. We've kept small-congregation pastors looking for screens and a quality praise band that "just might change everything." We've defaulted to endless efforts to get their patterns and practices just a little closer to something that never fit in the first place: *Hole. Putty. Paint. Repeat.*

And when these attempts were not enough, we turned to big-setting outposts. Even as worshipers longed for local faith communities, the answer was closer-to-home, multi-site worship from a big congregation hub.[8]

But it's what we didn't do that may be more important. We didn't look for distinctive strengths of small settings. And we didn't reimagine how to craft and curate worship with them—differently. *What are the local strengths of this size church and each community? What could we build*

---

8 Thom S. Rainer, "What Megachurches, Neighborhood Churches, and the Multi-site Movement are Telling Us," (https://churchanswers.com/blog/author/thomrainer/).

with them? What might the systems of streams and creeks—
not just the two mighty rivers—offer?

Curiously, this is not a new lesson for us. It's not the first time faithful, strategic folks have cherished the excellence of state-of-the-art armor. And overlooked what can be done with a slingshot and a few stones.[9]

---

9 1 Samuel 17. With thanks to Malcolm Gladwell, *Outliers: The Story of Success (Boston: Little, Brown and Company, 2008)* and *David and Goliath: Underdogs, Misfits, and the Art of Battling Giants* (Boston: Little, Brown and Company, 2013).

Chapter Four

Lesson 4: The Monkey Wrench of Incarnation
Seven Lessons for a Whole-Church Conversation

Replacing the measuring stick.

With mess, vernacular, difference.

And good news.

Christians have an inconvenient theology. We actually believe that the Holy Other takes on ordinary, temporary flesh. Just to show that we are lovable and redeemable.

And this divine work isn't some abstract proposition or gentle generality. The Incarnation of Jesus Christ insists on a jarring and *scandalous* specificity. With a savior who shows up during Roman occupation as a first-century, Aramaic-speaking Jewish-carpenter-turned-preacher from a backwater nowhere with a blended family. All for the rescue of a creation with its own intimate, impossibly diverse identifiers.

The Incarnation makes this point clear: divine love is not superficial infatuation. God searches and knows our details. All of them. And still comes for us. Every last one of us. Where we are. As we are.

Christian salvation doesn't try to escape the particularities of each context. It lives and works with them. So our ordinary, temporary flesh knows that salvation can live and work with us, too. In each community specifically. Not just most places generally. And because this is how God works, it's how the Church is expected to work, too. *Locally. Differently.* Even though attention to detail throws a monkey wrench into the elegance of one-size-fits-most programs. Even when that monkey wrench obstructs the simplicity of a single set of best practices.

The good news is messy. And it resists being reduced to good sense.

This lesson showed up at Pentecost when the Church received its incarnational work assignment. It came in a flaming hot mess of different languages. With so much chaos that public drunkenness was a perfectly reasonable explanation to bystanders. The Holy Spirit is apparently not bothered by differences among folks. Or worried about ideal settings. There was no divine attempt to tidy up the event with a single language. Or to fill the air with the smell of sweet incense rather than burning hair. Or to roll out a program with a well-coordinated advance team so others could replicate it later.

Instead, the Spirit sent this incarnational message: *Your work starts now. I'm sending you to all the people. So get used to mess and differences. That's where ministry always starts.*

It's a big lesson, one the Church returns to again and again.

This monkey wrench showed up in the last 500-year transition. During the last rummage sale.[10] We decided to give up worshiping in Latin because it didn't fit the

---

[10] See Chapter 1. Based on Phyllis Tickle, *The Great Emergence: How Christianity is Changing and Why* (Grand Rapids: Baker Books, 2008). With thanks to Ralph Adams Cram for this wry, apt metaphor.

incarnational mandate of local good news: *All the people, where they are, as they are.* So we changed our worship language to the vernacular—everyday words spoken by ordinary people in each place.

The change was inconvenient. And essential to our incarnational theology.

More recent liturgical reforms hurled the monkey wrench again. First, Vatican II dared to disrupt hundreds of years of settled patterns by calling for "full, conscious, and active participation"[11] in the liturgy by the ordinary folks in every parish on Earth. Protestants took aim with the monkey wrench shortly later. The result was a liturgical renewal with a call for greater lay participation and a theological reset. And this Protestant renewal produced those intertwining movements of praise and worship and contemporary worship.[12] Each movement paid attention to new details and identifiers. Each movement disrupted and innovated. Each provided fresh ways of connecting God and God's people. Here. Now.

And none of it has been convenient.

But the Church's mission has never been about convenience. The good news always arrives in scandalous particularity. The mission of the Church belongs in this particularity. Our worship should express it. Each faithful generation must translate divine love into the everyday understanding of each community—*local mess, vernacular, and difference.*

---

[11] *The Constitution on the Sacred Liturgy, trans.* Gerard S. Sloyan (New York: Paulist Press, 1964), around ¶ 14.

[12] Lester Ruth and Lim Swee Hong, *A History of Contemporary Praise & Worship: Understanding the Ideas that Reshaped the Protestant Church* (Ada, MI: Baker Academic, 2021).

So what does this have to do with small congregations?

Just this. We may be asking small churches to worship in a kind of present-day Latin. We may be guiding them to imitate the general worship language of large congregations. We may be expecting them to replicate the relevant expressions of another context—and build with someone else's set of specialty tools.

Perhaps we are seeking the convenience of one-best-way. Perhaps it's less overwhelming to share established practices of big settings rather than risk unfamiliar possibilities with small ones. But divine love can't be contained by our anxieties. It seeps into places that don't have proven plans. And it seeks to live and work with each setting—*differently, specifically, scandalously.*

So for the love of God, it may be time to put down the measuring stick. And pick up the monkey wrench—again.

But how?

Chapter Five

Lesson 5: In Search of a Small Congregation Toolbox
Seven Lessons for a Whole-Church Conversation

New clues from an old source—*aesthetics*.

The different rules of big-setting performance.

And small-setting participation.

A quick recap of the lessons: Worship matters because God shows up. Small congregations are not miniaturized big ones. Big congregations tend to drive most of our worship resources and expectations. But our incarnational theology insists on going local in each community.

So now what? Is there a distinctive small-congregation toolbox? Are there tools specifically for crafting worship in small settings—ones that work with local mess, vernacular, difference, and few additional resources?

The answer is yes, but we need to turn to an old source—*aesthetics*—to understand what's in this toolbox. And why we've been overlooking it.

The study of aesthetics is an old discipline rooted in philosophy. It explores how we perceive things. How we are affected by our senses. And how we decide what is beautiful or fitting.

Hang in there. This sounds complicated, but you already know it.

Different aesthetics are simply different clusters of sensory principles: patterns of sounds, sights, smells, and experiences that we recognize belong together and signal something together. These sensory clusters shape our expectations. They also cue our responses. Like the look of a Joanna Gaines farmhouse kitchen remodel: *Hey, call up the neighbors for an informal, elegant cookout!* Or like the expectation-response from the sound of fiddle music in two-four time: *Everyone just started two-stepping.* Or the expectation-response created by the solemn precision of a military funeral: *No instructions needed; we stood in silence.*

So what does this have to do with tools? Or small congregations?

Humans are incredibly sensitive to the power of aesthetic cues. For the most part, no one needs to announce aesthetic rules. We just recognize the patterns. For instance, we speak differently at a library than we do at a bar or t-ball game. We effortlessly understand that different settings call for different tools to be used for different tasks.

We also know that *mismatching* aesthetic tools and tasks can make things ineffective, awkward, or even damaging. Like holding federal court in a Magnolia-designed kitchen. *It won't work.* Or trying ballet in a honky tonk. *Big cringe.* Or answering work emails in the presence of a flag-draped coffin. *Gut punch.*

Plus, there's an important tools-and-tasks difference based solely on the size of the setting. Even apart from an event's specific purpose, we know small and large gatherings generally work differently.

Consider, for example, the difference between a 350-person formal wedding reception and a 35-person birthday potluck. Both are celebrations among friends and family with an order of events that will likely end with music and cake. But the aesthetic signals are enormously different.

At the reception, the very layout of the room reminds guests that they are witnesses of an event already scripted and prepared. Guests understand that they are largely passive observers. The head-table experts will guide the activities with prepared words and professionally recorded dance music.

In contrast, the potluck changes as each guest shows up. Guests understand that they are expected to help create the event—adding a dish, choosing a seat, and changing a conversation topic. Without prepared speeches. And with music marked more by enthusiasm than professionalism: *Happy birthday to you* . . .

No one has to explain these differences.

But mismatching the aesthetic rules of each setting would be disastrous. There would be little patience at a potluck if guests were instructed to sit in one place, follow along with a printed list of topics, and not wander through the kitchen.

Likewise, the reception guests would chafe at interruptions from anyone not seated at the head table. Or at guests asking the caterers if they need help with anything. Potluck guests might cringe at someone with a stack of prepared notecards for a speech. Reception guests might cringe if the best man tries to wing the toast.

You get the point.

The key to eliminating all that cringing is appropriately matching up aesthetic tools, tasks, and settings. And this is a foundational failure of how we've worked with small congregations.

We've been offering up big-setting tools for small-setting aesthetics. Mismatched aesthetics are why vibrant worship in big spaces with lots of people can feel awkward, ill-fitted, or worse—*pretentious*—in small settings. The sermon that soars in an auditorium may not work among pews with 50 folks. Big-setting resources—even excellent ones—can't simply be dragged and dropped into small settings. This is not because the small settings aren't doing them right. It's because the aesthetic principles they're trying to invoke don't fit. They have the wrong toolbox.

So, what's the difference in worship toolboxes? Some simple labels may help.

Large congregations depend on a big-setting *performance aesthetic.* They offer something beautiful for large gatherings—which come with large anxieties. So their toolbox requires big resources and power tools to coordinate, calm, and avoid chaos. They need teams of experts, clear authority, a predictable script, and high production values. The result is a kind of performative excellence. It works beautifully for big groups. But it comes at a cost: it risks turning worshipers into passive observers!

Small congregations can invoke a small-setting *participation aesthetic* instead. This toolbox avoids the need for extensive resources. And it also allows for the active participation of worshipers. It offers a different kind of excellence: a collaborative creation from the actual contributions of ordinary folks—not experts—with a flexible, up-for-grabs script. The event is more like a birthday potluck than a formal reception. It can change with each person who shows up. Worshipers are treated as active co-creators. The result is monkey-wrench friendly. With an atmosphere that more easily welcomes local mess, vernacular, and difference.

But there's an unexpected bonus of the participation aesthetic. It's called the "Happy Birthday Effect." You'll recognize it. After belting out "Happy Birthday" at a party, we don't seriously lament the performance on the drive home: *Oh, if only we had brought in a trained choir. Why didn't the altos practice more? We should have provided a professional recording.* Because the point isn't performing. It's collaborating. And collaborating quietly adjusts the aesthetic rules. Participation changes our critical engagement. When we participate, we are less likely to evaluate execution and more likely to experience belonging. A big bonus.

All of this suggests that the experience of creating something together can override the need for performative excellence. The participation aesthetic works with fewer resources and can provide a shortcut to meaning-making—*but only in small settings.*

One aesthetic is not better than the other. Both are rooted in the church's history. But each works with different challenges, strategies, and possibilities. We need both. But our big-setting performance practices have recently become muscular. And our small-setting participation skills have atrophied. We've mastered many of the big-resource production tasks of worship. But we've forgotten how to curate worship with conversation. Or summon the "Happy Birthday Effect" to make a joyful noise.

Can we find the small-congregation toolbox again? Can we relearn how to be artisans with what we find?

Chapter Six

Lesson 6: Training up Artisans
Seven Lessons for a Whole-Church Conversation

Experimenting, flailing, innovating . . .

And learning to work with small congregation tools.

Again.

This next lesson requires a story because it's not yet a set of quantitative facts. It's an observation that requires further exploration. And more conversation.

I noticed something intriguing while teaching a worship class to local pastors, most of whom served small congregations. When asked, "When have you experienced *excellent* worship," nearly all the pastors offered examples from large settings. They recalled the magnificent music that guided worshipers emotionally and expertly. They noted the lavish, beautiful settings, and thoughtful scripts for each transition, each set of words, and each anticipated response. The pastors recalled the centerpiece sermons with those just-right, carefully crafted phrases that revealed, challenged, and inspired.

Their answers highlighted the specialties of large congregations and periodic big events—not the specialties of weekly, local, small-setting worship. And no amount of putty and paint could replicate the answers to fit in their communities.

But then I noticed what happened when I changed the question: "When has worship been *deeply forming* for you?" The answers shifted. The stories were messier. The storytellers were not simply reporting an observation. They were describing their roles as protagonists. As active participants. They pointed to patterns of engagement over time that required additional context to understand.

I heard about a heightened sense of contribution: *I started decorating the chancel each week with the ordinary objects of our ministries; it told a story!* I heard about situations where something was up-for-grabs rather than scripted: *We just decided every child was qualified to be a liturgist.* The pastors also named local practices, signs, and symbols that required extended explanations: *We started worship with "mustard seed moments," our stories of how God shows up in the smallest of things.*

I wondered if the shift in answers revealed some hidden, overlooked, or forgotten strengths of small settings. Over the past decade, I started looking for these strengths. A seminary invited me to curate worship for their small community housed within a large church. We experimented, flailed, collaborated, and learned. A denominational conference allowed me to develop a series of yearlong worship workshops for small-congregation pastors and laity. We innovated, stumbled, explored, and followed up together over time. We reached for new vocabulary to express the differences we were experiencing.

And over the past decade, I noticed distinctive characteristics among the pastors with vibrant small congregations. They worked differently. They were less deferential to the measuring stick and more observant of their individual communities. They wielded the monkey wrench and summoned local gifts. They focused on participation density rather than performative excellence. They invited ordinary playfulness rather than polished expertise. Worshipers were subjects and protagonists in the divine "meet-up." They were collaborators and co-creators.

Worship planning started with an inquisitive look at their individual congregations and communities. The pastors asked, "How could we craft worship from *these* gifts and interests? What could worship look like?" The approach was more like making *Stone Soup*[13] than beef wellington. The work began by looking in the pantry rather than buying all the required ingredients from a recipe card. Most small-congregation pastors followed a traditional order of worship. *But they populated it with local mess, vernacular, and difference.*

The pastors shared some of their examples:

- One church invited a troubled kid from the neighborhood to play the role of Paul for a month of sermons.

- Worshipers brought personal items to the altar representing their burden or thanksgiving.

- Alongside the sermon, someone baked bread to illustrate John 6. Another time, someone tuned a motor to explain the importance of spiritual disciplines. And during another service, someone

---

[13] Marcia Brown, *Stone Soup* (New York: Charles Scribner's Sons, 1947).

tended to a demanding, orphaned calf to remind everyone that God's shepherding is not an easy pastoral abstraction.

- Several congregations celebrated with the music, photography, and dramatic arts of local high school students who had no idea that their gifts could be worship gifts.

- Some relearned how to belt out faith songs with the energy of "Happy Birthday" at a loved one's party.

None of these examples would win an award for excellent performance in music, visual arts, or drama. But maybe that was the point. No one was *performing*. No one was creating a polished product. Something new was happening—or maybe something really old. Somehow the practices were summoning a different set of expectations and responses—a different *aesthetic*. And the raw, use-whatever-we-have, hands-on, invitation-to-participate of this aesthetic vibrated with Gospel.

The good news showed up gloriously with imperfect, ordinary participation rather than perfected, expert performances.

Throughout our workshops, we remembered that the prophet Miriam didn't have a script when she picked up the tambourine. We discussed how sermons were unpredictable "table conversations" before they became polished pulpit proclamations. And we remembered that Jesus did an old-new thing with some unleavened bread among friends.

The point is that ritual knowledge never arrives fully formed. It emerges in messy practices by real bodies using whatever they have. By rivers, on plains, and in living rooms.

So, from there, we worked to consciously rejoin our own tradition.

At first, we identified a few distinctive small-setting strengths that would *not* work in big settings.

1. A collaborative way of planning worship
2. The power of hands-on tasks in worship
3. Actual conversation!

More strengths kept popping up.

4. The ability to include local signs and symbols, not just the general, universally-recognized "meaning-makers"
5. The ability to treat a wider range of local talents as worship offerings
6. Leadership that sought partnerships, not proprietorships
7. Expanded possibilities for proclamation that included laity

We identified seven strengths in all. But we suspected there were more. This was a start. Our work involved more mess than formula because the practices looked different in each setting. Then came the realization that all these strengths shared five common characteristics. So these five characteristics became a worship aesthetic for these thriving small congregations. Here are those five shared qualities:

- Increased worshiper participation and collaboration
- Heightened hands-on contact for worship work
- Greater dependence on lay leadership

- An order of worship resourced from local gifts and interests

- An unsettled script that could be shaped by those present

The seven strengths were simply tools for unleashing this five-part *aesthetic*.

And this aesthetic did something unexpected. It replaced resource-intensive requirements for high-production worship with lovingly diagnosed, ordinary, local contributions. It marked a path for monkey-wrench-friendly, incarnational, collaborative worship.

So maybe participation was more than a "good fit" for small congregations. Maybe it was an *advantage*.

Chapter Seven

Lesson 7: The Participation Advantage
Seven Lessons for a Whole-Church Conversation

A practical and theological case:

Curating worship with the strengths
of small congregations.

For the whole Church.

A participation aesthetic is a good fit for the limited resources of small congregations. But is it good for anything else? Could it actually be a worship *advantage*?

The answer is yes—maybe even a big yes—with both practical and theological support.

Let's start with the practical stuff. Many disciplines study participation as a powerful tool hardwired in humans. Education theory, leadership studies, neuroscience, business and consumer sciences, linguistics, philosophy, hermeneutics, and sociology all recognize that participation prompts something in us. Participation facilitates and accelerates tasks like connecting, creating, learning, and problem-solving.

Participation is also a potent meaning-maker. The Harvard Business School offers intriguing confirmation in its research study, "The 'IKEA Effect': When Labor

Leads to Love."[14] The name of the study points to a big box store that is both beloved and notorious for DIY furniture kits. But the scope of the study is much bigger. It explores how humans respond whenever "some assembly is required."

What happens when we participate or collaborate in making something? Specifically, does hands-on work affect our valuation of the work product? Do we work for what we already love? Or do we love what we have worked for?

Spoiler alert: We love what we have worked for. Participation, it turns out, is a powerhouse of formation.

Here's how the study worked. Participants were given basic tasks for which they had no expertise or particular interest. Like building IKEA boxes, folding origami creatures, and assembling Lego models. The results were not the marvelous creations of master artisans. Sometimes the researchers even left out important steps in the instructions. But on completion, all works were displayed.

And this is where the study gets clever. A bidding system was set up for the finished projects. A currency was provided to both the hands-on participants and a group of hands-off observers. Everyone bid. The researchers then compared the bids of those two groups— participants and observers. Which group assigned a greater value to the work?

You can probably guess the results. The hands-on participants bid more. They experienced the boxes, birds, and buildings as inherently more valuable. Work created a greater impact ("love") than mere observation

---

[14] Michael I. Norton, Daniel Mochon, and Dan Ariely, "The 'IKEA Effect': When Labor Leads to Love." *Journal of Consumer Psychology* 22, no. 3 (Hoboken: John Wiley & Sons, July 2012), 453–460.

of the finished project. Touching, crafting, and creating increased a sense of connection. The researchers explored the contours of this effect, but the bottom line is this: "Labor leads to love." Our hands-on work—*participation*—forms what we love, value, and desire.

The study's results should be unsurprising in a tradition where liturgy is the work of the people. We've known it all along. Worship is our "forming labor." It is the building, folding, and assembling of our Christian identity.[15]

This is where the theological support joins in with a big amen!

For Christians, participation has always been more than a practical concern. After all, it's baked into the good news. Incarnation is God's participation *with* us. And in worship, God invites us to participate right back. To grow the relationship. To draw closer.

We are not simply passive objects of divine love. We are invited into a mutual exchange of receiving, contributing, and co-creating the kingdom among us. We don't *watch* the salvation story; we are *activated* into it. Richard Rohr reminds us that there is no faith without this deep sense of participation. We don't just believe in something. We are a part of something. The Christian life is embodied by praxis, not passivity.

In the Middle Ages, we thought of worship as a theater production. The priests were the actors. God was the prompter giving them the scripts and cues. And the people were the audience. Simple enough, right?

---

[15] E. Byron Anderson, *Worship and Christian Identity: Practicing Ourselves* (Collegeville, MN: Liturgical Press, 2003).

The plan seemed settled and convenient. Until some disrupters suggested another way—with reformations that eventually became *the* Reformation. A faithful innovator named Søren Kierkegaard suggested a different model for worship: The people are the actors. The up-front leaders are simply prompters. And God is the audience.

This model is now our theology. More than fifty years ago, the Roman Catholic Church boldly claimed that worship work requires "full, conscious, and active participation" of the people."[16] Protestants followed suit. Our liturgical renewal seeks out this kind of participation.[17]

The definition of "full, conscious, and active participation" is still not clear. We don't have an official list of regulations and accepted practices. *Of course.* And with the oversight of that incarnational monkey wrench, the list would differ from place to place anyway.

But this much is clear for the whole Church: Liturgy is an active collaboration of clergy and laity. *Together.* It is the robust work of all the people. The people are subjects, not objects, of this labor. And the goal of participating is not just more ritual action—more work for work's sake. It is about being drawn deeper into the mission of the Church itself. Forming what we love, value, and desire. To lead us into the very heart of God.[18]

So here's the wrinkle. The participation emphasis creates a curious paradox for the Church today.

---

[16] The Constitution on the Sacred Liturgy, trans. Gerard S. Sloyan (New York: Paulist Press, 1964), ¶14.

[17] E. Byron Anderson, *Common Worship: Tradition, Formation, Mission* (Nashville: United Methodist General Board of Higher Education and Ministry, 2017), 121-140.

[18] With thanks to Ron Anderson and Don Saliers for more than they may ever know!

The *practical* challenge of managing big groups has introduced a *theological* challenge. In large congregations, the roles of worship leaders have become increasingly important. And the roles of worshipers have become more passive. Worship has become the work of the prompters, not the people. Worshipers have become a target audience, not essential actors.

Not surprisingly, current conversations about worship participation sound partial, passive, and weak. The theological concept gets reduced to something practical—like how to keep the worshiper's attention. As if participation is mere intellectual assent. And not a fully embodied response or praxis.

But perhaps this is where small congregations can make a precious offering. To the whole Church. [19]

The distinctive strengths of small congregations are rooted in the characteristics of participation. Small congregations are poised to take on this labor-into-love. They can help replace partial, passive, and weak participation. They can explore full, active, and robust participation instead. They can become local laboratories, indigenous innovators, and good news diagnosticians—*again*.

This will require a change in perspective. Understanding the seven strengths requires turning things upside down—or maybe right side up. But the change in perspective should ultimately feel faithful and

---

[19] Yes, there is a participation difference between small and large congregations. "Smaller congregations have high levels of member commitment . . . with a greater percentage of member participation . . . with participants [giving] more money per person . . . and more likely to volunteer." Aaron Earls, "Small Churches Continue Growing—but in Number, not Size," Insights: Church Life & Ministry (October 20, 2021).

familiar. Like the handle of a well-worn monkey wrench. Unleashing small congregations is not a call to change our orders of worship. Rather, it's a call to broaden how we populate them to include margins and edges. It's a call to expand how we curate our worship forms with local mess, vernacular, and difference.

And it's a call to let small congregations lead these forming labors. For the advantage of the *whole* Church.

Let's talk—and listen.

PART 2

DEAR SMALL CONGREGATIONS, THERE IS ANOTHER WAY

Seven Worship Strengths of Small Congregations

Prelude: **The Participation Advantage**

Strength 1: **Stone Soup Worship Planning**
Rebecca's Story

Strength 2: **Hands-On Contact**
Diane's Story

Strength 3: **Worshiping with Conversation**
Paul's Story

Strength 4: **Employing Local Signs and Symbols**
Steve's Story

Strength 5: **Including Co-Creator Gifts**
Alan's story

Strength 6: Leading with Partnerships, Not Proprietorships

Amanda's story

Strength 7: Widening the Word

Heidi's story

Ready to dive in?

- Start by reading the introduction to this book. The whole Church needs you in this conversation.
- Don't read this book alone. It's meant for clergy and laity to work together.
- Treat this like a workbook. Each chapter includes five questions to help you make plans—again, *together*.
- There's also a bonus section at the end called "Worship Wonders," with three unexpected theological conversations. Each fits your work and will serve the kingdom of God everywhere.
- Set a schedule for reading and meeting. Some congregations may meet weekly for seven to ten weeks to cover the chapters. Others may cover (and practice) one strength each month.

Note: All stories in these chapters have been shared by actual small-congregation clergy and laity. *Alleluia!* **But some details have been combined or adjusted to help with efficient sharing.** *Also Alleluia!*

Chapter Eight

PRELUDE: THE PARTICIPATION ADVANTAGE
Seven Worship Strengths of Small Congregations

Why It Matters and How You Already Know it

Dear Pastors and Laity,

Before jumping into the strengths, it's important to start here. With the *participation aesthetic* (or the *participation advantage*). Because it's the goal of all the distinctive strengths of small settings. And it's a big challenge for big congregations.

Don't worry, though. You know more than you realize. Even though the terms *participation aesthetic* and *performance aesthetic* may sound curious and pretentious, you already recognize and practice the difference. You know that participation is powerful. It transforms our perceptions and experiences.

Remember gathering for a potluck birthday party? The conversation shifts and expands with each new guest. The table changes with each dish added. Stories are told (and retold). At some point, a cake appears. Candles are awkwardly lit. The whole group bursts into a round of "Happy Birthday" with no rehearsal. The event ends with the warmth of silly stories, renewed relationships, and full bellies. And afterward, no one thinks, *Ugh, we should have hired a professional choir.*

That's called the "Happy Birthday Effect." And it's the gift of the participation aesthetic—that full sensory experience created when each person contributes to and affects an event. When something is up for grabs, unscripted, and dependent on each guest, there can be a heightened sense of belonging and meaning-making. And this sense of belonging and meaning-making is ultimately more important than pulling off perfect four-part harmony. Participation matters. It changes the encounter.

It's worth rereading the "IKEA Effect" summary, too.[20] This study by the Harvard Business School proves an essential human trait: we love the things that require our hands-on labor. We desire them more and find them more beautiful. Participation shapes us in ways that are more powerful than mere observation. It's a principle recognized by more than just furniture-assembling, birthday-singing folks.

Some years ago, a Hollywood actor startled his interviewer with this principle.[21] He had a lengthy list of big-budget, big-screen credits, but when the reporter asked what kind of work he preferred, the answer was quick: "Community theater." *Wait.* Not the excellence of big screen productions? "You prefer low budgets, little rehearsal, small audiences, amateur directors, crews, and casts? Really?"

"Definitely."

---

[20] See Chapter 7.

[21] I've tried desperately to find this public radio interview. I remember it aired while folding laundry and matching socks on the dining room table. Apparently, those are not helpful search terms.

He explained. With the big screen, something happens to the audience as the lights go down. They read the opening caption, "New York, 1939." And they flip into performance-observer mode: *Okay, prove it. Impress me.* They look for excellence, check for flaws, and monitor the performer. The movie production must do all the heavy lifting: convince, inspire, and move.

In community theater, on the other hand, someone carries out a broomstick handle with a handwritten sign taped to the top. Everyone leans in to read it together: "Oh, it's New York, 1939 *tonight*—and we get to go, too!" There's an anticipation of seeing *our* local talent. No one minds the from-my-closet costumes. No one is worried about selling the production rights. The work is done together. A connection is made. There's a real-time conversation between the actor and the audience. They affect one another. The audience changes the event. There's a sense that something is happening in this very moment.

The two experiences—making a blockbuster movie and acting in a local playhouse—are very different. For this actor, the enthusiasm of that second experience somehow exceeds all the budgets, teams, and perfect takes of a cinematic performance. The possibility of participation summons something. And for the actor, this "something" outshines performance and production excellence. Hands down.

This "something" is the participation aesthetic. And it's an advantage for small settings—*your* advantage.

Large settings have no choice but to pursue a kind of performance excellence that requires resources, experts, and scripts. It's the only way for large settings to communicate with large crowds effectively. But it's not the only way for small settings. Participation is a powerful alternative. It lights up our brains with anticipation (*my presence matters*) and warms our hearts with intimacy (*we did this together*).

No wonder participation is at the heart of so many strengths of small congregations. But the significance of participation is not just practical. It's also theological. For Christians, *liturgy* literally means the work of the people. And *all* people are meant to be working folks. Not just the up-front leaders and production staff. It's a lesson passed down from the Reformation. The worship leaders are simply prompters. The people are the actors. And God is the eager community theater audience.

Large congregations are at a disadvantage in embodying this theology. To manage large groups, the worship leaders must take on the primary work. And their leadership signals to worshipers that they are an *audience*.

But small congregations don't have this disadvantage. They can practice "community theater" and "potluck party" worship. They can figure out the rules of *presence* rather than *production*. They can call upon everyday gifts and real-time connections.

And here's the amazing news: it can resemble the patterns of the Early Church. Remember that unscripted, enthusiastic bunch? They gathered together in the presence of God for conversation and a meal together. They weren't passive observers of a performance but active participants in the holy drama, leaning in. *Oh, the kingdom of God! And we get to go, too!*

Here's the **goal**, the participation aesthetic for small congregations:

- Increased worshiper participation and collaboration
- Heightened hands-on contact for worship work
- Greater dependence on lay leadership
- An order of worship resourced from local gifts and interests
- An unsettled script that can be shaped by those present

And here are the seven distinctive **strengths** that will get you there. These are the practices that unleash the power of participation in small congregations (and don't generally work in big congregations):

1. Stone Soup Worship Planning

2. Hands-On Contact

3. Worshiping with Conversation

4. Employing Local Signs and Symbols

5. Including Co-Creator Gifts

6. Leading with Partnerships, not Proprietorships

7. Widening the Word

If you've taught children, hosted a potluck, celebrated a birthday, or simply lived among your neighbors, these strengths should feel familiar.

But there's also a big challenge. We have so much performance worship in our heads and on our computers that it may take experimentation and practice to remember this other "old-but-new" way. You'll have to plan differently—clergy and laity together. It's not about creating a better production. Instead, it's about figuring out how to signal the permission-giving "Happy Birthday Effect." And creating more opportunities for every last person to collaborate and contribute local talent in worship. Then watching for the lights to come up on the kingdom of God among you.

Start the Conversation

1. Share the story of an event when you were an essential, cherished participant or collaborator. How did it feel?

2. How is this experience different from being a passive observer of a performance?

3. In what ways does your congregation's worship signal a performance aesthetic? In what ways does your congregation call for a participation aesthetic? Be specific.

4. Imagine ten different ways someone can participate in worship—even if they are not a longtime member.

5. Name ten different gifts/interests/hobbies you see in your community—not just your congregation. Can you imagine worshiping with them?

Chapter Nine

Strength 1: Stone Soup Worship Planning
Seven Worship Strengths of Small Congregations

Maybe you've heard it said that for lavish worship, congregations must have a "Worship Design Team"—experts gathered to design, script, rehearse, and coordinate the event. In detail. Every. Single. Week.

But what if small congregations have a more powerful option—one that expands participation, emphasizes lay leadership, ends the burnout of meetings, invites local gifts, and heightens anticipation? Because something is up for grabs and each worshiper just might affect it for everyone?

They do. It's called Stone Soup Worship Planning.

Catch a Glimpse

A month at a time, the pastor makes a one-page guide with the following information for each week:

1. The scripture

2. A short thematic statement

3. A related image, sign, symbol, or question

That's it. Then the pastor recruits lay leaders—*just for that month*—for specific tasks. Like decorating the altar/chancel/sanctuary, offering children's worship, reading scripture, or creating a short drama. The pastor hands off the guide to each of the lay leaders and encourages their interpretations and gifts: *Share whatever you have.* No meetings or rehearsals. Just anticipation about what might be made together on Sunday.

Hear the Story

It took a few weeks at her new appointment, but Pastor Rebecca recognized three persistent worship complaints. The first complaint was, "I'm burned out." It came from the same few people who took care of everything week after week. The last pastor urged them to try a "worship design team" model to liven things up. There was enthusiasm at first: *Maybe this is how successful churches do it.* Then came the burnout. The meetings to brainstorm, plan, coordinate, refine, and rehearse became too much. They ended after one quarter with exhaustion. And a vague sense of failure—again.

The second complaint was, "*You* fix it!" This one was aimed at Rebecca. Two appointments ago, the pastor did everything himself. It was easier that way for him and the congregation. But it was also a little dull to watch. No new members showed up. And no old members invited anyone: *Why would they come?*

The third complaint took some careful listening. It was *felt* more than spoken: *What if we can't?* Around every conversation about worship was a nagging worry that there was not enough. Not enough people. Not enough ideas. Not enough resources. Not enough time or talent. They feared decline, closing, and a "takeover." In response, some people fiercely resisted change. Some kept looking for that right resource to bring back young people: *If only we had a band.* Some blamed the economy, the denominational leadership, and the building. But all the responses had this in common: *Maybe we just can't do it on our own.*

Here's what Pastor Rebecca didn't do. She didn't rally the burnouts to push harder. Or assure them that she could fix it. And she didn't focus on weekly worship scripts that would increase the performance value.

Instead, she spent her time learning all the gifts, interests, and talents in her congregation *and community.* Especially the hidden ones that didn't usually show up on Sunday mornings—things like photography, painting, baking, and flute playing.

She wrote a simple, one-page worship guide for each month. It included the weekly scripture, a thematic statement, and an anchoring symbol. Then she set out recruiting and encouraging:

I noticed that you. . . .

Here's a guide. . . .

I wonder if you could help us in worship?

Sometimes nervously, Rebecca said yes to every gift, interest, and talent offered. She handed out tasks—even on Sunday mornings: *Could you fill the baptismal font and invite people to remember this gift?* She involved visitors: *Would your child like to carry in the light of Christ?* And she recruited others even when she could do the task better or more efficiently.

It didn't happen overnight, but something changed. It started with a retired educator who was not even a church member. Rebecca asked the educator to decorate the chancel area for a month. At first, the educator balked: *I'm not really a church person.* But with a combination of love, permission, and persistence, the educator said yes. Then decorated with a creative passion. Each week was a surprise, a thoughtful interpretation of the worship guide. Bales of hay from the field outside were stacked as an altar and decorated lavishly for a Thanksgiving celebration. The narthex became a welcoming living room. She wanted to decorate for another month.

Word got out. Others began offering their decorating ideas for the altar. They interpreted the guide with a combination of items from the sacristy and the local thrift store. Worshipers sometimes added personal objects as they arrived. Some youth in the community began writing a drama each month. A farmer who attended the church years ago showed up with animals on Christmas Eve. There was a buzz in the community grocery store each Monday: *I wonder what they'll be doing this week?*

The congregation renamed Pastor Rebecca's "Stone Soup Worship Planning" model. Instead, they called it "Get the Ball Rolling." Because that's all they want her to do. Rebecca sends the guide to all interested parties. Just to get the ball rolling. Then the laity take over. They interpret, recruit, and imagine. The anticipation builds through the week. Pastor Rebecca uses a flexible order of worship and leads it like a gracious host welcoming beloved guests to a growing potluck party—one that honors the Holy One who hosts us all.

Two years later, worship participation is denser. More people do more worship work. The path between the church and community is better worn. Rebecca doesn't hear, "We're burned out," "*You* fix it," or "What if we can't?" Even in a struggling, shrinking rural community, there's a sense of abundance. And that retired educator, who wasn't a church member, is exploring a call to ministry: "I never knew that my gifts mattered. It turns out I am a church person. Now I want to share that with others."

Rebecca keeps saying yes—still, sometimes, nervously.

Connect the Dots

Stone Soup is a popular European folktale. It's told in different ways around the world, but the essence is this: A stranger shows up in a small village. The stranger is hungry. So are the villagers, but there seems to be nothing to eat. Everyone has so little. All are starving and wary.

So the stranger starts the hospitality by setting out a giant pot and politely asking for a large stone. He claims to have a delicious soup recipe. As the villagers gather to watch, he builds a fire, fills the pot with water, and drops in the stone. He stirs it with delight and anticipation.

After tasting it, the stranger announces that it's good but would be much better if only there were a little carrot to add. Eventually, a villager produces a hidden stash of a few carrots. The stranger savors a taste and announces that it would be even more delicious with a little onion or some meat. A villager returns with the ingredients. Over and over again, the traveler declares the soup good and wagers that it could be even better if. . . . Over and over again, the villagers bring out what seem like meager offerings on their own. Together, however, they create an enormous, nourishing soup that feeds them all. Starting with just a stone.

The recipe for delicious soup isn't a list of ingredients. It's an invitation to imagine and help. That's the goal of this style of worship planning. Invite, imagine, help. With this model, the pastor is the stranger. And the pastor doesn't arrive with an apron, a cooler of ingredients, and the recipe for beef wellington. Instead, the pastor arrives with a simple guide and the ability to stir, encourage, add, and declare good all those gifts hidden away by hungry folks. Somehow through the process, the fear of scarcity transforms into a feast of abundance.

But it's important to back up and make clear what Stone Soup planning is—and, more importantly, what it is not. Stone Soup planning is a way of *curating* worship that works well in small settings. It is not an order of worship. That's a separate exploration with a wealth of helpful resources from our tradition and your denomination. *Instead, Stone Soup is a way of populating any order of worship with local gifts.* It treats these gifts as good, valued—and even capable of revealing the sacred. It emphasizes an embodied celebration of the incarnational good news.

Let's be clear. This hand-it-off planning method won't work if your goal is replicating a script for a perfect performance. It's also ill-advised for gatherings larger than one hundred people. But if you're in a small setting ready to increase participation and its deep formation, the Stone Soup method works. In fact, with some time, tending, and practice, it works wonders. This tool is one of the surest ways to signal the participation aesthetic.

To summon its *advantages*. And to grow an abundance of worship gifts from your congregation and community.

Take note. There may be resistance—from both clergy and laity. Pastors may chafe at the uncertainty of the Stone Soup method. They will have to plan differently. Lay leaders who take care of *everything* may scoff at its inefficiency or feel fired. They may anxiously wonder: *Aren't our jobs difficult enough without juggling all the chaos? Won't it all be amateurish? Who will control the worship?*

Who, indeed?

These are anxious questions, more appropriate for formal wedding receptions than potluck parties. They point to concerns of a performance aesthetic. They also skid over some theological bedrock. Our salvation story is anchored in surprise. The Spirit delights in it. Our worship practices it in each cycle of the Christian year: *Just wait until you see what God does with chaos, a manger, a bunch of amateurs, and an empty tomb.* As we encounter the stories again, efficiency and familiarity yield to awe.

An interesting thing happened in the initial series of worship workshops that revealed this planning method. The most resistant pastors and laity became the biggest converts to Stone Soup planning and the participation aesthetic. Something happened as they redirected their energy toward identifying, recruiting, and encouraging lay gifts:

- The call and response of worship got bigger.
- They discovered more gifts hiding in plain sight.
- They permitted new ways that didn't depend on their control and excellence.

In short, the pastors were liberated, too. Worship became something done *with* them, not *by* them. It was the work of God's people together.

Get Practical

This collaborative work starts with the pastor. Well in advance, the pastor thoughtfully and prayerfully lays out the month or liturgical season. Many pastors report that this kind of monthly or short-term planning makes sermon preparation easier. Just as importantly, however, it allows for richer lay participation.

In creating the simple worship guide, some pastors may follow the lectionary. Others may create their own thematic series. But there's an additional resource to consider: short, small-group studies, Bible studies, or special-topic studies. While not specifically imagined for worship, these work well in small congregations using the Stone Soup method.

Here's how. The pastor chooses a study and then assigns a chapter, scripture, and dominant theme to each worship week. Copies of the study should then be given to lay leaders for their planning. Worship doesn't become a study. Instead, the study gently coordinates the focus of worship. It's a resource and inspiration for all: *How might we worship with this?*

After the pastor creates the simple guide, the work shifts to recruiting, encouraging, and handing off tasks. This is crucial work. And there are two important reminders. First, the soup-making traveler savors the broth and imagines how good it would be with just a little. . . . The soup maker does not mandate: *Bring onion, finely diced. Yellow, not red. Exactly three cups.* The goal is to give gentle direction and generous permission. To show that their gifts truly matter.

Second, the soup-making stranger doesn't say, *Oh, and this task is yours until Jesus returns.* Let's face it. Small congregations have a reputation for sticking people with jobs. But more people will say "yes" when they trust that the job comes with a set term. And more people will take risks in sharing their gifts in worship a month at a time. The rule is pretty simple. For the first year, recruit laity for specific jobs one month at a time. Pastors may want to start the recruiting work, but laity can also notice, encourage, and invite.

So what kinds of worship jobs are you recruiting for? Start with these basics:

- Children's worship (the children's sermon or other participation by children in worship)
- Visual arts (decorating the chancel area—or the whole sanctuary!)
- Dramatic arts (offering the good news in an unexpected way)

Too overwhelming? Pick one for starters. Try a once-a-month approach for the dramas and visual arts, but don't be surprised if a hunger grows for more jobs. Then turn to include gifts from your community. Can the local photography buff take pictures of where she sees God in your community? Can the flute player at the high school offer a song of celebration? Can a home baker prepare a sourdough starter and a plan for delivering bread?

Pastor Vern and his wife, Cindy, noticed a hunger-for-more at their three-point charge in rural Nebraska. Two years later, they started a whiteboard system at each church to keep up with all the participation.

The whiteboards lay out four worship weeks at a time. Each week includes the scripture, a symbol, a character, and a theme. Pastor Vern added a secondary theme and a question to ponder each week. The whiteboards also include spaces to write in the names for a growing list of worship work: leading children, reading scripture, decorating the chancel, acting out a part, sharing a short testimony, offering the benediction, visiting those who could not attend, offering a surprise art. They had to keep adding lines for names and jobs. The boards change monthly. And the names are written with a dry-erase marker—not a Sharpie.

Then they noticed something interesting. Over time, the path between the community and the church was getting well-worn. Folks started dropping by the churches to check out the whiteboard for that month: *What might happen, and when can I help?* The whiteboards aren't hidden away in an office. They're visible to everyone. They serve as an unlikely statement of faith: *You matter. Worship is collaboration. God's doing something with all of us together. What can you offer? We can't wait!*

Start the Conversation

1. Share a moment when you've experienced deeply
   meaningful worship in your congregation. Tell the
   story with lavish detail. After everyone has shared,
   what do you notice about these stories?

2. Review the story of Pastor Rebecca. Does your
   congregation share any of the three complaints? What
   are the unspoken messages about worship for you?

3. How has your congregation planned for worship in the past? Name the various ways. Have some been better suited for *performance* rather than *participation?*

4. Change comes with resistance. What kinds of resistance did you experience reading about Stone Soup planning? Too chaotic? Not enough help? No volunteers? Name them aloud. Then, as a group, answer this: How does the Gospel speak back to these fears?

5. Start imagining: How could we encourage a well-worn path between our community and sanctuary?

Chapter Ten

Strength 2: Hands-on Contact

Seven Worship Strengths of Small Congregations

Maybe you've heard it said that meaningful worship must be carefully choreographed for repeatability at 10:30 and 12:00. And, of course, everyone knows that this requires two categories of folks: active experts and passive observers. It just does.

But what if small congregations have more powerful, deeply forming options to make worship a hands-on experience for everyone? What if the work of the people could be the actual work of the people?

It can.

Catch a Glimpse

Treat worship like a full-body contact sport. Get worshipers' hands on as much stuff as possible. As often as possible. Provide options. For example, invite worshipers to decorate the altar, write, paint, doodle, or respond by placing objects at the altar. Think like that creative teacher loved by everyone in grade school. Heighten the participation possibilities for each worshiping body.

Hear the Story

Something kept unsettling Pastor Diane about the man's answer. It was strangely familiar. She replayed the words again in her mind. He declined her invitation to come to Sunday worship. That much she expected. But then he offered something quite unexpected: an explanation. He said these words: "Sorry, but it's tough for me to sit through worship. I'm restless. I don't really get it. That's not how I work."

Back in her office, the familiarity of the explanation hit her. She had spent fifteen years teaching before becoming a pastor. That meant she spent fifteen years looking for the signs of "I don't really get it." More importantly, she accumulated fifteen years of figuring out alternatives for "that's not how I work."

Pastor Diane's spirit was certain of this much: everyone learns differently. There's no single lesson plan that fits every learner. Different learners have different needs. A worksheet might be fine for some, but others might need to sort colorful blocks by hand. Or turn their ideas into pictures or stories. Restlessness is not a flaw. It's an invitation to find another way. To include—and enjoy—movement and touch. *Contact.*

She also knew this. The full-body approach she used in her classroom did not benefit only a few. It enriched the experience for everyone. Even those perfectly pleased with passively listening. So she thought maybe the same principle might apply to worship. It did. Pastor Diane brought her teacher's compassion and wisdom to church. She decided worship should include hands-on options. Contact. Movement. As often as possible. She decided that all the learning differences among folks could make worship richer. For everyone.

She started by changing how the worship space was prepared on Sunday mornings. Instead of ensuring the table was perfectly set before everyone arrived, she stacked the altar cloth, cross, candles, and other objects on the back pew. During the prelude, she invited people to prepare the sanctuary together. As an act of worship. The first few weeks were a little awkward. Worshipers worried about doing it right.

Then something interesting happened around the second month. People began making prayerful, even creative, choices. About draping the fabric, placing the candles, or bringing in the cross. They lovingly arranged the objects related to the scripture theme. Pastor Diane couldn't predict—*no one could predict*—exactly what the worship space would look like. There was a new excitement about this hands-on preparation. She noticed that some people started checking ahead for the worship theme. And bringing objects from home to include.

More importantly, while preaching, Pastor Diane noticed that this decorating changed the worshiping. Those who had prepared the altar kept looking at their work—*their offering*. Their eyes moved from her. To the cross. To whatever they had touched. And back again. They kept returning to the thing they had touched. It touched them, too. This simple contact affected how they heard her. And perhaps how they listened for God. The hands-on experience shaped a new conversation for the worshiper: *Maybe my flowers matter. Maybe that nest from the backyard fits. Yes, maybe God is listening for me, too.*

And this participation created a long-term effect. Pastor Diane noticed that months later, worshipers would refer to "that Sunday when I placed the globe on the altar." As if it was still vivid for them. Because it was. Their hands-on participation made the experience more memorable somehow. Having touched something, they were more deeply invested in meaning-making. Contact helped move them from passive to active worship work.

Not a big surprise, really. But, this observation unleashed Pastor Diane's imagination. She began experimenting. And inviting the congregation to join the experimenting:

- What if the children could place their Sunday School projects in front of the altar during the opening hymn?
- What if we set up a table in the back with art supplies: clipboards, simple easels, colored pencils, and colorful clay? So worshipers could create instead of just sit?
- Why don't we let worshipers carry in the bread and cup? And maybe set a dinner table?
- How can everyone have the opportunity to respond with bodies and not just thoughts?

Diane was careful to make sure these hands-on jobs were open to all. Not just lifelong members and typically-abled bodies. But also the kid who just moved in next door. The single woman who worked nights most of the year (who cried as she set the communion table). And the usually homebound man who wanted to carry in the cross from his wheelchair.

A funny thing happened. After a year or so, the hands-on nature of worship seemed to call back some people who had quit attending. Like that man who said, "I just don't get it." He never sat still in a pew for an hour. But he started finding ways to worship hands-on. He helped organize the Drive-Your-Tractor-to-Church Sunday. He brought in new chicks at Easter to show the children. He bundled up canned goods and whatever was being harvested to place in front of the altar—an offering. And Diane noticed that he kept glancing at his work as he paced the back of the church: *My offering.*

When COVID forced the community to find other ways to worship, they were ready. A lay leader packed boxes with altar cloths, candles, crosses, the church china, and various ordinary ministry items from around the building. The man who paced helped drop them off at homes and nursing facilities. Even places where they knew the boxes might never return. It was worth the risk. Because they knew the power of contact.

Instead of passively listening to virtual worship, the congregation encouraged a different way. Each person could set up a worship center, a reminder of God's presence with each body, even when our bodies are apart. They shared pictures and stories of this work of the people, too.

It highlighted something they already knew: Worship is not something to watch. It's something to do. With your hands and body. In worship, the things you touch allow the Spirit to touch you.

Connect the Dots

It's worth repeating: participation matters. Enormously. And hands-on contact is an intense form of participation. It's not just *thinking*. It's *experiencing*. Hands-on participation moves meaning-making from a between-the-ears moment into a full-body encounter. And neuroscientists, great teachers, and Christian educators agree that full-body encounters form us deeply.

Noted neuroscientist David Eagleton unpacks this marvel.[22] He explains that our brains are not fixed pieces of equipment with a simple on-off switch. Instead, our brains are "livewired." Their circuitry is always changing. The eighty-six billion neurons in each brain are not fully preset. They respond, grow, and adapt. *Continually.*

So what triggers this respond-grow-adapt pattern? Concrete interactions with the world. Things like social engagement, conversation, and play. They are the strategies that "[allow] the colossal machinery of the brain to take shape from a relatively small set of [genetic] instructions."[23] Interactions make us. And among the most powerful interactions are motor and sensory feedback. *Contact.*

What we do with movement and objects sets up feedback loops. These feedback loops integrate our internal and external worlds. *Touch, move, feel, experience, integrate, repeat.* And these feedback loops then literally write our neural circuitry. We are formed by our bodily contact with the world.

So, the richer the patterns of motor and sensory feedback, the richer the possibilities for formation, right?

But neuroscientists are not the only ones who recognize the value of motor and sensory feedback. The field of education has its own testimony to the importance

---

[22] David Eagleman, *Livewired: The Inside Story of the Ever-changing Brain* (New York: Pantheon Books, 2020).

[23] Eagleman, *Livewired.*

of full-body-contact learning: Universal Design for Learning (UDL).[24]

The word "universal" does not mean one way for everyone. It means everyone can be included. Diane was right. A single lesson plan won't work for every learner. Different learners have different challenges. Perhaps more importantly, different learners have different strengths. They may work best by moving, ordering, creating, or touching. Not just hearing and viewing.

The UDL principles also insist that the stakes are high for paying attention to these differences. If we don't want to discard learners who don't fit, we need the flexibility to include a variety of learning styles. Full-body sensory contact can be a powerful tool.

Insightful teachers recognize this power. They can see a third-grade girl who wriggles in her chair and feels stupid because she can't memorize the multiplication tables. They can have her bounce a ball as she learns to recite them. Miraculously, the combination of movement and math triggers a new response. A new pathway. She gets it. She's not dumb. She's a kinesthetic learner who needs to add physical activity to write her best neural circuitry.

Insightful teachers can also see a boy who resists reading. Until he finds a subject he loves and is invited to build the novel's setting out of cardboard and colorful paper. An effective teacher can see a middle schooler who can't remember class conversations. Until the teacher presents him with new colored pencils and asks him to draw what he hears.

---

[24] https://udlguidelines.cast.org.

Think back on what happened with the ball, cardboard, and colored pencils. The objects simply created contact. They facilitated formation with motor and sensory interaction. But there's even more good news from educators. This formula doesn't simply benefit a few struggling kids. It enriches everyone's learning. All kids. All adults, too. Even the uncomplaining learners. It helps every *body.*

This is where your small-congregation strength shows up, led by a marching band! Large-setting worship has to limit the unpredictability of all those hands and bodies. So worshipers are all handed the same basic job description: *watch, listen, sing, stand, sit. But please don't touch.*

Small settings, however, can do things differently. You have the advantage of flexibility. You can imagine lots of job descriptions for the work of the people. You can set up worship as a workshop rather than a lecture hall. Think about the difference. With two thousand people, the lecture hall event must limit participation. But with seventy people, the workshop can intensify participation. And grow neural circuitries with hands-on options for experimenting, interacting, arranging, touching, drawing, building, creating, and presenting. You can be the experts of worship with the liturgical equivalents of bouncing balls, cardboard, and colored pencils.

And contact is not just good neuroscience or education. It's also sound theology.

Renowned theologian and author Don Saliers reminds us that worship itself is our primary theology.[25] The

---

[25] Don E. Saliers, *Worship as Theology: Foretaste of Glory Divine* (Nashville: Abingdon Press, 1994).

important stuff of Christianity is not simply information but how we enact what we know and experience in bodies together. We don't merely think *about* the liturgy. We also think *with* it.

Our faith has followed Universal Design for Learning before there was UDL. Remember the ministry of Jesus. He didn't run a classroom with a single lesson plan. He found roles for blind beggars and wandering children. Efficiency was not the first priority. Yes, there were sermons, but they included the cues for contact: *Consider those lilies of the field (brushing against your legs) . . . Take and eat this . . . Stretch out your withered hand . . . Let her bathe my feet in ointment. . . .* His ministry could not be reduced to mere ideas.

The good news is not informational. It's transformational. It requires actual bodies and insists on re-forming the feedback loops of real people. It requires incarnation—which is, itself, the mystery of contact.

Just look to our sacraments, those most powerful truths of the Christian faith. Sacraments integrate the divine reality with our own. And they require nothing less than contact. For two thousand years of practice, we *feel* baptismal waters on our skin and *taste* bread and wine on our lips. Our sacraments are not mere ideas. They are full-body, sensory-motor experiences. And meaningful worship is not an intellectual exercise. Rather, worship dances with touch, image, and movement. And it should be filled with lilies, food, movement, balls, blocks, colored pencils, and flexibility for every last learner in God's kingdom.

This is the strength of small-congregation ministry.

You can listen with the ears of Jesus to folks outside your doors who may be quietly mumbling, *I just don't get it.* You can insist that the kingdom not discard people who learn differently. You can find messy, inefficient, different jobs in worship. Because you know this work belongs to every *body.*

Get Practical

So, where to start?

Remember, you don't have to do *everything* to do *something.* Pastor Diane had the right approach. Add contact a little at a time. Experiment. Encourage. Observe. *Grow.*

You can invite a few folks to get started. But eventually, try to give the big "y'all come" and see who responds. Pastors should hand off contact work as quickly as possible to interested laity (including children). And don't be surprised if lay leadership for this work comes from outside your regular members. In fact, seek new folks. For some worshiping learners, this is a long overdue answer to "But that's not how I work." Continued practices of contact will bring outsiders in.

Decorating the altar and chancel area is a great place to start. The altar serves as a stage for playing out the salvation story without words. It's capable of unleashing quiet, profound conversations between the cross and whatever we put around it. So try this. Set out some primary faith symbols—the cross, Christ candle, Bible, bread, and cup. Include some additional objects—everyday things, local signs. Add color with formal altar cloths or informal drapes of fabric. Include glorious, shiny fabric that suggests the High Holy. And rough, ordinary cloth that points to the Right Here. Then invite someone to arrange, order, imagine, or tell a story with these objects. Let worshipers play at thinking *with* the liturgy.

Something miraculous can happen when we strike up these silent conversations. Without spoken sound, the altar alone can preach and testify. It can say things like, *Over even this, Jesus is Lord.* Or, *God is here with you, just as you are.* Or, *Remember, God provides lavishly.*

Ready to add a second simple contact practice? Add other objects of hands-on ministry in worship. Invite people to place them around the chancel area. *During worship.* For instance, the gardeners who tended the church's flower beds that week should bring their work gloves and hoe forward. The Bible study group can place their book and notes on the altar. The children can display art projects from Sunday School or home. Nursery workers can bring a tub of toys to clean each week for safe childcare. Homebound persons can send a picture of their home altar and worship seat. Worshipers can stack the chancel area with the paper goods and diapers that will stock the church pantry—after the prayers of blessing for those who need them.

Contact with each of these items matters. Placed before the cross, they whisper deep truths. And repeat them throughout worship. They form us with messages like these: *Your offering matters because you matter. Your work is part of the salvation story. Who else should be here? Yes, I'm sending you!*

One pastor adopted a silver tray practice. Before each gathering of worship, meeting, or study, she wrote out jobs on sticky notes: *Arrange the chairs. Offer an opening prayer. Prepare and serve coffee. Find a way to include everyone in the conversation. Check the bathroom supplies. Invite us to remember our baptism!* She placed the notes on a tray. And as folks arrived, she invited them to choose one. To participate.

Ready for a bigger leap into contact practices? Try an Arts Sunday. Set up an enticing table in the back of the sanctuary. Fill it with art supplies. Small jars of colored pencils. Packs of markers or crayons. Clipboards with blank paper. Maybe even watercolors, small canvases, and easels. Then invite worshipers to work during worship and create something. You can give them a specific assignment like "What does it mean to feast?" Or let them decide. Toward the end of worship, invite them to bring the creations forward and display them around the chancel area. Treat them as precious offerings. Because they are.

Some congregations schedule an Arts Sunday once a quarter. Others set out "doodle supplies" (clipboards and colored pencils) every week for those who choose. Some include things like clay and pipe cleaners to enrich passive listening. Some include notecards and pens for worshipers to write responses or take notes. The key is that the activity must be hands-on. And treated as belonging to worship.

But there's a crucial theological caveat to this work. Once someone intentionally places or arranges something in worship, leave it. It should not be repositioned or "fixed" to make it look better. Period. Otherwise, with the potency of ritual action, you risk harm. Someone may hear, *You weren't up to the task.*

In worship, nothing could be further from the truth. Instead, trust that the cross is powerful enough to have a grace-filled conversation anywhere and with anything in its presence. Don't diminish that conversation.

One pastor shared the story of a child who carried in the big altar Bible. Unable to easily lift it to the altar, she carefully arranged it on the floor in front. Sideways. A long bolt of fabric spilled over the altar onto the floor. So she wrapped it around the Bible, tucking it in like a baby. The reverence of the act spoke to everyone. The Bible stayed put. And spoke.

They heard.

Finally, along with the altar decorating and Arts Sundays, just get contact-creative. Imagine hands-on worship jobs for particular people: *Can you set the communion table like a celebration with dishes from home? Can you fill the baptistry and invite other worshipers to splash and remember as they arrive?* Note: Kids are great ambassadors for this task! *Can your body dance, direct, or sculpt? Would you like rocking chairs in addition to pews?*

Your ideas for contact, movement, and sensory feedback for each worshiping learner are important. So find more. Imagine. Experiment. These are holy tasks. Contact practices can form bodies deeply in the marvelous mysteries of our faith. And you happen to be perfectly positioned for growing this kind of work. For the whole Church.

Start the Conversation

1. Look up Universal Design for Learning (UDL) on the Internet. How does it invite your curiosity? Wonder aloud together: Does our worship offer options to passive listening? What do you notice in the principles of this approach?

2. Interview an expert. Invite a creative teacher to help identify barriers to different kinds of learners. Are there ways that more contact could be included? Brainstorm three simple ways that could offer worshipers more contact. Try these for at least six months.

3. Pause a moment for prayerful consideration. As you read about contact, neuroscience, and education practices, did someone's face come to mind? Who might enjoy an opportunity to do things differently? Who might benefit from more flexibility in worship?

4. Where might you experience resistance to adding more contact opportunities in worship? Do you feel a nagging resistance yourself? How does love speak to that feeling? What specifically does it say?

5. Set aside practicality for now. Don't talk about dates, limitations, or conflicts. Instead, imagine an Arts Sunday—playfully, lavishly, delightfully. Share these ideas with one another. Try this format: *Wow, I wonder what would happen if. . . .*

Chapter Eleven

Strength 3: Worshiping with Conversation

Seven Worship Strengths of Small Congregations

Maybe you've heard it said that including conversation in worship is simply too unpredictable, messy, and anxious. Worship works best when everyone agrees on the right call and the proper response. With no surprises or talking back—thank you.

But what if God is not afraid of conversations where each person can be heard? What if God yearns for them? And what if small congregations have a deeply forming worship strength because they can practice wondering, questioning, and talking back together?

Like the Early Church.

Catch a Glimpse

Build in the opportunity for authentic calls and responses in worship. Erase the divide between passive pew-sitters and active leaders. Find ways for all worshipers to add their words, ideas, motions, and emotions. So all can help shape the worship. For example, ask a question for the call to worship. Invite short responses to the scripture. Or continue worship around a dinner table. So the communion liturgy includes an intimate sharing of table talk.

Hear the Story

Pastor Paul counted more than a dozen conversations on Monday morning. Typical. The owner of the hardware store chatted about the high school team. He also wanted to make sure Paul picked out the right caulk. (He hadn't.)

At the diner, the familiar crowd handed out the usual humor. With plenty of weather speculation. Pastor Paul heard about a new grandchild, a neighbor taken to the hospital in the night, and the family across from the church struggling with another eviction notice. At one end of the counter, there was talk about quietly leaving another box of groceries on the front porch for the family. One woman worried that it did not seem like enough. The needs in their community were many. And multiplying. On Paul's way out the door, the diner's owner whispered a plea. To keep praying for her nephew's battle with addiction. The diner was where everyone went to know what was going on. And to be known.

That evening, Pastor Paul met with his administrative council. More conversations. They were always ready to talk things through. Sometimes to death. Often inefficiently. Paul came to respect the gentle everyone-has-a-voice chaos of the meetings. He recognized that the conversations mattered. They weren't mere words. They weren't simply information. The conversations created relationships and belonging. Even when there was disagreement.

Conversations were how folks challenged, connected,

adjusted, laughed, lamented, and collaborated on everything from home repair to personal despair. They might not be efficient. But they were definitely important.

Except during worship.

When worship started, conversations stopped. Completely. Like the silence of the county court in session. The signals seemed clear to folks even without being spoken: *Defer. Don't chime in. Know your place.* So interactions ended. Along with some of the enthusiasm.

But Pastor Paul recognized that worship is fundamentally a kind of conversation. Call and response. God calls; we respond. We cry out; God answers. Then we repeat the pattern with each other. Together. Worship is interaction, collaboration, co-creation, and relationship. It is about listening and being affected. Answering and affecting each other. It's a mutual exchange. Not a courtroom hearing.

So Paul decided to experiment. If conversations were so important to this community, maybe they belonged in worship. Like they did for the Early Church. Maybe worship could feel more like the diner than the courtroom.

There were plenty of worries to work through first: *Where did real-time conversations fit in their order of worship? How could he invite worshipers to participate? How could he facilitate conversations as worship work— not just diner chatter?* After all, no one taught that in seminary. And there was, of course, the big fear: *What might happen without the usual, fully settled script?*

Taking a breath, he remembered that surprise is built into our faith story. It's some of the Spirit's best work:

What do you mean a baby will save us? How is Jesus not still dead? You're really going to trust the Church to take on the divine mission?

And what happened next is what always happens with experimentation. Some things worked. Some things didn't. Some parts were awkward at first but became cherished over time and practice. The congregation learned together.

First, Pastor Paul included conversation in the call to worship. It was high time they quit reading words in unison like zombies. And it was time to include folks who couldn't see. Or read easily—or at all. So he started with his weekly worship guide from Stone Soup worship planning. And he added a simple, coordinating question for worshipers' responses:

Weekly Scripture: Exodus 17:1-7 (God provides for the grumbling, wilderness-wandering Israelites.)

Opening Question:

When have you received something unearned and deeply needed? How did it change you?

Or later, this example:

Weekly Scripture: Matthew 11:28-30 (Jesus' invitation to weary folks)

Opening Question:

Remember a time when you have struggled or been worked to the bone. How did it feel? Or how *does* it feel?

Reflection:

"Jesus said, 'Come to me, all you who are struggling hard and carrying heavy loads, and I will give you rest'" (Matthew 11:28-30 CEB).

Deepening Question:

Who in our community is struggling hard or being worked to the bone? How might they feel?

Closing Reflection:

We are the eyes and hands of Jesus. Join his compassion in responding, "Come to me, all you who are struggling hard and carrying heavy loads, and I will give you rest."

In the first week, there was more noise from crickets than worshipers. Then there were a few weeks of the same people talking. Too much. Pastor Paul learned to build in silence after the questions. So worshipers could reflect first. One soft-spoken lay leader put pens and notecards in each pew. So worshipers could jot down a response before sharing. Like she did. And it worked. More folks participated. They also began thoughtfully responding to each other.

The practice changed their worship. The gathering was still reverent. But it felt more like God had a chance to meet the real folks—the ones who showed up at the diner.

Initially, Pastor Paul felt obliged to oversee all responses like a master of ceremonies. But soon he realized this kind of leadership was unnecessary. He could trust the Holy Spirit, the people, and the liturgy to gather all the words. The good news is comfortable with messy interactions. God is gracious enough to receive our words. So we can graciously receive each other's words.

Some weeks, Paul decided to invite conversation after reading the scripture. As a way to hear it more deeply:

> *What questions do you have about all those "blessed" pronouncements from Jesus' Sermon on the Mount?* [26]

Sometimes he asked what phrases intrigued them. Or troubled them:

> *Is there one of those blessed categories that you don't think belongs?*

Some weeks he invited worshipers to share only a short response:

> *What phrase do you remember from the Apostle Paul's letter?* Or, *Name the emotion that rose up when you overheard Jesus tell the religious leaders to give Caesar whatever was Caesar's.*[27]

In other weeks, he invited them to spill out stories:

> *Have you ever seen someone still seeking healing after years of quiet suffering? Have you ever been that person?*

After each conversation, they read the scripture again. Followed by silence. It usually resulted in a new kind of engagement. A deeper worship encounter. With less

---

[26] Matthew 5:1-12.

[27] Matthew 22:15-22.

paper shuffling and fewer bathroom trips. Pastor Paul also noticed that worshipers often returned to these conversations after the benediction. *Surprise!*

So he kept experimenting with conversation in other parts of the worship order. For instance, as a call to prayer:

How does our prayer draw us deeper into the needs of the whole world, not just our own?

How can we include the fullness of life in our prayer—everything from ecstatic joy to the deepest agony?

In other weeks, he added a conversational response to the sermon, like the week on the raising of Lazarus:

How does Jesus unbind and free you?

How can we unbind and free others in our community and our world?

Paul also tried conversation *as* the sermon (but stay tuned for more on this in Strength 7: Widening the Word).

The experience was humbling. Pastor Paul realized that he knew more about perfecting his own words than including words from other worshipers. He needed to keep experimenting. Because something heartwarming was happening. Over time, there was more participation. But there was also a deeper sense of shared vulnerability. Among the worshipers. And before God. *Transformation?*

Some weeks, the congregation was surprised by awkward, raw stories. Like when the diner owner's nephew, Carl, showed up. During the call to prayer, he shared his battle with mental illness and drugs. Some worshipers squirmed in the pews. Pastor Paul knew this kind of conversation would never happen in a large setting. But it belonged in worship. Their work together was never meant to be confined to cheap happiness and polite words. Carl had something to offer in worship. And he belonged, too.

Over time, the children also participated in worship. They learned that their words mattered. They belonged, too.

The interactions weren't polished. But Pastor Paul noted that awkward moments sometimes felt especially holy. Like they had stumbled into the mystery of just how far God is willing to go to be with us. And everyone was in on it together.

Conversation—a genuine, vulnerable call-and-response before God—is powerful.

So no one was surprised when Carl kept showing up. Most Sundays. No one was surprised when more folks began offering their own words. Or when more worshipers invited neighbors—*even children!*—who had never known that their words mattered to the church, too.

And no one was surprised when Carl asked to be baptized. Or when he celebrated his baptism with an enormous tattoo on his arm the following week, "So my street friends can see that I belong to God now." He wanted his tattoo to start conversations with people who knew more bad news than good. Its flaming rainbow of colors around a cross was his response to a benediction conversation: *Where will you go this week? How will the world see that you've been changed by divine love?*

Connect the Dots

Worship is fundamentally a conversation. The call and response between God and the gathered for a mutual exchange. We generally expect lavish worship to include ritual, order, and symbols. But for small congregations, it can also include the power of *actual* conversation thoughtfully curated in the order of worship.

Is this really such a big deal?

Well, *conversion* is an important word for Christians. It's the whole point of the good news. God doesn't leave us where we are. Divine love meets us, moves us, and turns us around. It changes us. And draws us deeper into the heart of God. We are converted.

And this is where things get intriguing for small congregations. Because the word *conversion* is related to another word that small congregations know well: *conversation*. The words share two important roots. The "con" part means "together. And the "vers" part (*versare* in Latin) means "being turned." So conversations meet us, turn us around, and change us. Together. In conversation, people don't simply deliver unrelated lectures and go their separate ways (ideally). They listen, respond, and adapt. They affect each other in real-time.

Of course, this makes conversation risky stuff.

Asking a genuine question unsettles power. It shifts control. From the questioner to the responder. The interaction leaves things up for grabs. After a question, the responder might derail or redirect. Or ignore the engagement entirely. Or need time to answer. Or lash out. And the questioner must wait to receive the response. Listening with curiosity and empathy.

Allowing an impact. Not simply proceeding with a preplanned presentation.

Conversations allow each party to affect the other. So the exchange creates a peculiar kind of vulnerability. And this vulnerability, it turns out, is an important tool for building relationships and growing communities. Vulnerability opens us up. It allows us to connect and respond to others. It invites us to know and be known.

Perhaps this is why our Bible consistently shows God in the conversation business. Our scripture is packed with divine questions. Recognize these?

Who told you that you were naked?

Where is your brother Abel?

Hagar, why are you crying?

But who do you say that I am?

Mary, why are you crying?[28]

Questions seem to be one of God's favorite tools for incarnational engagement. God seeks conversations. But why? Surely the author of creation knows the answers, right? Why ask? Perhaps it's this pattern again. Because questions invite conversations. And conversations initiate vulnerable exchanges. And vulnerable exchanges grow relationships and communities.

It's the familiar dance of divine love at work. God speaks creation into existence, then offers to have a word—*The Word*—with us. To restore the good creation, God seeks to talk *with* us, not just *to* us. And God nudges us to talk with each other, too. The Pentecost

---

[28] In order from Genesis 3:11; Genesis 4:9; Genesis 21:17; Matthew 16:15; and John 20:13.

people didn't simply speak in tongues. They also asked questions, listened, and responded: *How is it that we hear each of us . . . What does this mean?* The first act of the Church was conversation.

Perhaps it's not surprising that this theological theme also shows up in our own neurobiology. After all, we inherited the divine image—the very source of all this *con-versing.* Scientists recognize that conversation lights up our brains. And that different kinds of conversations light them up in different ways. For different tasks.

One group of scientists breaks down conversations into three levels.[29] Level 1 is **transactional conversations**. These are simple exchanges of information. The interaction is limited to sharing basic facts: *Where is the nearest bathroom?*

Level 2 is **positional conversations**. These conversations include opinions and advocacy. But the interaction is focused on "selling our ideas" rather than allowing influence by another person: *I want a seat by the window because. . . .*

And then there is Level 3, **transformational conversations**. These are the most complex and vulnerable exchanges. They're also called "co-creating conversations" because both parties shape them. And both parties are shaped by them. The interaction involves "asking questions for which you have no answers, listening to the collective, discovering and sharing

---

[29] See, for example, Judith E. Glaser, "The Neuroscience of Conversations: A Deep Dive into the Fascinating World of Conversations," *Psychology Today* (Sussex Publishers, LLC, May 16, 2019).

insights."[30] It seeks more than just information. And it invites each person to affect the other: *How did you experience. . . ?*

The brain payout for these transformational conversations is big. They summon our greatest creativity, our deepest listening, and our most profound change. Yes, these are the conversations that turbocharge conversions. And yes, Jesus specializes in transformational questions. Like the bold road-to-Damascus invitation: *Saul, why do you persecute me?* (Acts 9:4). Or his gentle nudge for the disciples to connect the dots of abundance: *How many baskets of leftovers did you gather?* (Mark 8:19-21). Or his pointed plea for mutual vulnerability: *Do you see this woman* (Luke 7:44)?

You could add many more questions to this list. Maybe there's one that started your life-changing, together-turning conversation with God.

For Christians, conversations are essential. We need them to encounter the good news, to practice it, and to be changed by it. They belong in worship. And small congregations can learn to employ them lavishly. On behalf of the whole Church. *Ask. Listen. Connect. Transform. Share.*

Get Practical

Fear often gets in the way of worshiping with conversation: *What if I don't know how to respond? What if worshipers say too much? Or too little? Or interrupt with something wildly inappropriate?*

---

[30] Glaser, "Neuroscience."

These fears are not new. Reread Corinthians 11-14 for a reminder that Christian gatherings have long struggled with imperfect worshipers. Accept that there isn't another kind of worshiper. Then try these ideas.

- First, as usual, craft the weekly worship guide from the Stone Soup chapter. It will coordinate and focus the worship work. Identify the scripture, theme, and an anchoring image, sign, symbol, or question.

- Then start small. Conversation in worship is not an anything-goes pursuit. It should serve and deepen the worship. Begin by curating worship in one element of your usual order, like the call to worship or call to prayer. Or as the preparation to hear the scripture. Later you can experiment with its gifts elsewhere in your order of worship.

- Working within the worship guide, craft worship questions in advance. Write them down word for word. Practice them to see what responses they invite. Revise.

- If worshipers are quiet, invite them to write responses. Or, you might start with a transactional question: *Where do you go when you need a break?* Or a positional question: *Who was right—the prodigal son or the brother?*

- Pay attention to how the three kinds of conversations (transactional, positional, and transformational) work in your community. Learn the local signals and etiquette for them.

- Don't try to include a transformational question in more than one place each week. Too many can create a sense of whiplash or mere noise. These kinds of questions come with great vulnerability and require significant time, patience, and *listening*.

93

- Seek out resources that teach group *facilitation* skills. Not just *presentation* skills.

- Increase the quality of silence in your worship—one minute at a time. Conversation requires listening, and listening requires space and stillness. Be honest about your anxiety with filling the silence.

- Create a safe place for conversation. Watch for how people are excluded, corrected, or filtered. Then prayerfully respond and adjust. Work to treat outsiders like precious insiders—like God does.

- Make room for honest words about pain. Don't insist on cheap cheer. Our psalms assure us that there are no topics that can't be brought before God! Practice that assurance.

- Include children. Generally, if something works for them, it works better for everyone. Remember that for Jesus, they were not an interruption. Children were the very expression of the good news! They show up on the honored guest list for the kingdom of God! Practice adding them to your celebrations.

Start the Conversation

1. Is your congregation like a diner where people come to be known? Or like a courtroom where people come to be told? Does it work differently for members and visitors?

2. Give some examples of recent transactional and positional conversations. Then share a transformational conversation: *When were you changed or transformed by an interaction?* Describe what happened.

3. How is worship like—or not like—conversation for your congregation? How do people participate in a call and response with each other and God? What levels of questions are asked and answered?

4. What are the specific barriers (usually *fears*) to including genuine conversation in worship? Name them out loud. Then imagine how the good news might talk back to each.

5. Review the "Get Practical" section together. Name one worship practice you'd be willing to explore with conversation. How could you create a safe place for all worshipers to respond in your congregation?

Bonus question: Can you name the transformational question that started (or continues) your conversation with God?

Chapter Twelve

Strength 4: Employing Local Signs and Symbols

Seven Worship Strengths of Small Congregations

Maybe you've heard it said that great worship requires great words, each thoughtfully researched, crafted, and delivered. Because nothing is more powerful than the right heartfelt words.

But what if there were things vastly more powerful and memorable than words? There are: signs and symbols. And what if small congregations have a distinct advantage because they are not limited to general signs and universally recognized symbols that fit the scale of big settings? Small congregations can invoke local signs and symbols—even small personal ones—to explore the scandalous mystery of grace right here among us.

Catch a Glimpse

You probably already have an altar or table in the chancel area. Worshipers most likely face it together. Like a stage where the good news is played out. And it probably already displays some High Holy meaning-makers. Like a cross, lighted candles, and a large Bible.

These symbols start big conversations without a single spoken word. Because they point to who God is and what God does for us. But these messages can be even more powerful when you add *local* signs and symbols. So look closely for the Right Here meaning-makers in your community. Then place them alongside those precious, mysterious, High Holy symbols in the chancel area. And listen for the incarnational conversation.

Hear the Story

Pastor Steve was the youth leader at a big steeple church. The staff was large. The budget was large. And the possibilities for ministry felt enormous. So he turned his full creativity toward translating Christian talk into teen talk. He explored the good news with their practices, experiences, language, humor, and *stuff.*

It was a wonderful and exciting time. Then God did a familiar, unsettling thing: God nudged (or maybe threw?) him into ministry. Within a few months, Steve found himself enrolled in seminary, learning new depths of Christian talk, and serving a small, rural congregation. Of mostly older adults. By himself.

The first time Pastor Steve walked into the small sanctuary, he still saw things with his big-church goggles. The chancel area was too small for a praise band. It didn't have nearly enough electrical outlets. Oh, and there were no screens or projectors. He had been warned not to ask about a "tech team."

He then investigated a room behind the sanctuary that held altar cloths, candles, communion sets, seasonal signs, and symbols. *Ah, the sacristy.* He smiled and recognized the same basics from his big-steeple church. Except that the big-steeple church had larger candles, longer altar cloths. And an enormous advent wreath stunningly designed to be seen from the back row. Big churches had to go big. The scale of worship required it to match the size of the space. Little, personal, ordinary things would go unnoticed.

Standing in the small sanctuary, however, Steve remembered something. Another holy nudge, perhaps. Some of his most powerful moments in youth ministry had nothing to do with big, stunning setups; elaborate drum kits; and auditorium-sized events. The most meaningful experiences were smaller. More intimate. They weren't about producing the perfect moment with all the right words and decorations. These powerful moments were more about recognizing God among imperfect, everyday moments. When *little things* were noticed. And sometimes became big things. Beyond words.

For instance, one trip transformed the youth group. They traveled to a city on the opposite side of the state. Using only public transportation and eating only at soup kitchens along the way. They sought solidarity with those they sought to serve.

The final destination was a large, rundown church that served an unhoused population. The entire event was inconvenient, unglamorous, and *exhausting*. The youth stood in line for stale bagels with the rest of the precious folks. They cleaned and organized dusty rooms in the church. They got up at five each morning to walk the city—like their unhoused neighbors. Their guide explained that all area shelters required people to leave at that hour. To get them moving and start their days.

Practically, this meant walking city blocks in the dark. And figuring out where they could find bathrooms, shelter, and food until the shelters opened again.

So the youth did this too—somewhat irritably.

The guide pointed out heavy black plastic bags along the city blocks. They looked like trash. But she explained that they were actually coveted possessions. The trash bags carried, hid, and protected valued items. They provided ground cover for resting on the sidewalk. And with three simple rips, the bags could be worn like a tunic to stay warm and dry.

The youth group gathered in a small, dusty chapel for prayer and processing that night. Steve had asked each person to bring an item to share from the day. Something that pointed to what they had experienced: *Where had they seen Jesus? What had they noticed with the eyes of Christ?*

One girl had saved a piece of stale bagel. She placed it on the altar: *I guess we have what we need.* Another youth found a tiny flower growing between cracks in the sidewalk: *There's beauty here, too.* One boy brought a crumpled piece of newspaper that had been given to him in case the public restrooms were out of toilet paper: *That dude was looking out for me!*

Then one of the members who had been especially quiet shared his story. Before foster care and adoption, he had spent years living in shelters. This was not a new experience for him. He already knew about early morning walks and black plastic trash bags.

He took a bag he had found on the sidewalk. It had the rips of a tunic. He set it on the altar, too. Then, with the surprise of the Spirit, someone had the great idea of hanging it on the big, shiny cross that hung from the ceiling. *The Savior wearing this tunic of last resort.*

Steve didn't have a polished sermon. He didn't need one. He simply asked someone to read John 1:14: *And the Word became flesh and lived among us.*

They all sat silently in the presence of this mystery. The High Holy was right there.

This worship experience marked a turning point. Even once the group was comfortably back home, they gathered and offered up ordinary things they'd noticed. They placed them on a corner table in the youth room. Under a small cross. Sometimes with a black trash bag laid out reverently as an altar cloth. Steve would read a scripture passage. The signs and symbols helped interpret it even without a lot of words. Steve noticed that the youth no longer talked about faith as an *idea*. Now it was a *way of life.*

Somehow, in the presence of the cross, their ordinary objects were transformed. They launched holy conversations. Not with just words. But with *The Word* intimately speaking with teens in a youth lounge.

Steve decided to take these lessons to his small congregation. Perhaps the problem was not the electrical system. Or lack of staff. Or all those big-church practices that didn't work here. Perhaps the problem was that he overlooked an enormous advantage of small-scale worship: the ability to let sacred symbols speak directly to these folks. With their practices, experiences, language, humor, and *stuff.*

He started simply. And a little awkwardly. He asked

worshipers to bring signs of where they had seen Jesus that week. Or to bring objects pointing to a conversation they were already having with God. No one participated at first. Steve was sure the look in their eyes meant something like, *Ah, another young pastor with new ideas.*

Then an older woman known for her hospitality told him she had an idea. The following Sunday, she quietly brought in her lace tablecloth and china set. These were the special dishes she brought out to serve anyone just moving to town. During the prelude, she decorated the altar like the table at one of her "everyone's welcome" dinners. A complete place setting. A familiar blue goblet. She carried in the communion bread on the usual brass plate. But moved it to the dinner plate. She filled the goblet. Lit the candles. And gestured with wide arms: *This invitation is for you. A meal prepared for you. Welcome!*

Three months later, they had a handful of helpers eager to interpret the weekly worship themes on and around the altar. Pastor Steve had coffee with them each week. One helper hadn't attended worship for two years. Another had never set foot inside the church. All were intrigued by Steve's invitation to express big sacred truths with small, ordinary objects.

On World Communion Sunday, they gathered everyday household plates from every group that had settled in the community. *Please celebrate with us.* Someone loaned her great-grandmother's serving dish from Czechoslovakia. Another offered an aluminum TV dinner tray. All plates were placed on a gleaming, white cloth under the cross. And all were loaded with loaves of bread offered in communion. Then shared in a potluck that felt like a feast. *The body of Christ here. Among our neighbors. With all creation!*

During Lent, worshipers brought signs of things that got in the way of their relationship with God. A stack of old bills. A cracked mirror. An old calendar filled with appointments and scribbles. The picture of a parent who had died. Some worshipers explained their offerings in a sentence or two. Others simply left the object on the altar in silence. The enormous cross stood among the objects. It insisted on a new conversation: *Nothing can keep you from the love of God!*

On another occasion, after serving chili at a local festival, worshipers brought signs of where they glimpsed God outside their sanctuary. Each worshiper offered a sentence or two and placed an object by the cross. One woman dragged out a yellow plastic child's chair from the old Sunday School room. She set it in front of the altar. Then moved the Christ candle onto its seat: *Jesus welcomes children. We've got to get back in the game!*

Somehow the cross transformed all of the ordinary objects into a proclamation. About neighbors. And God's kind of care. So the child's chair stayed beside the altar that year. Each week it nudged a conversation deeper than words. Then came the words. By the end of the year, the congregation was partnering with an afterschool program.

Steve recognized that something powerful was happening—without adding a single electrical outlet. There was a power to the local signs and symbols. They deepened the worship explorations and led these folks deeper into the heart of God.

Connect the Dots

First, a quick lesson explaining the difference between signs and symbols. A *sign* represents something else. It's an object that stands in for another thing or idea. Signs work like a math equation with an equal sign. *This* equals *that*. The yellow chair was a sign for children.

But *symbols* work differently. Symbols are powerful and deep meaning-makers. They have the ability to speak more than any set of words. In fact, symbols can't be reduced to words—even lots of really good words. Symbols always mean more. They defy equations. They always *point* to something bigger. They work like an *arrow*—rather than an *equal sign*.

Consider the symbol of our flag, for example. It doesn't equal the United States. When a flag is draped over a casket, ceremonially folded, and presented to a waiting family, it isn't the equivalent of a return address. It points to an indescribable system of relationships, values, sacrifices, histories, and personal stories. *Bigger. More.* And the lump in our throats reminds us that some meanings can't be fully explained.

We need symbols to do the heavy lifting.

Try explaining the meaning of the cross. Or the kingdom of God. Or baptismal waters. Or communion bread and wine. We can describe these symbols in many ways. But we can't pin them down to a single definition. They will always mean more. They will always connect us to more. They will always point us to a reality greater than our words and imaginations. This makes symbols essential tools for worship.

In worship, we encounter the One who is always bigger

and more. *The Great I Am*. The One who is beyond words. *Yhwh*. We need arrows that point to a mystery rather than equations that can be solved. So we gather around a table with bread and wine. Or face a cross. Or carry in a Bible. Or the light of Christ. We invite these symbols to transform our worship conversation. *Bigger. More.*

And this is where big congregations may face a limitation. They need objects that fit the scale of the chancel area—things that will be seen from far away. Additionally, they may need to stick with least-common-denominator symbols—things that are easily recognized by a wide variety of people. Small congregations don't have these same limitations. You can invite worshipers to interact with our faith symbols. You can use local symbols of all sizes. You can play out the salvation drama in the chancel area by placing small, personal, ordinary objects by the cross.

But there are two crucial reminders. First, remember that local signs and symbols are not simply about making the sanctuary pretty or well-decorated. They are working tools of the liturgy. Their job is to unleash the good news with a power beyond mere words.

And finally, no one can simply create symbols, local or otherwise. Their significance is too big to be manufactured or manipulated. But they can be *recognized* as they emerge. Like that black plastic trash bag that revealed the fullness of the good news itself. *More* than any words could capture. Or like that yellow chair. It started out as a sign representing children. But over time, the chair was transformed by the cross in worship and loads of interactions with children and their families. Until it also became something more: a local symbol that pointed to God's provision. To their own faith and mission. To the kingdom of God among them and yet to come. *Bigger.*

Put your faith symbols to work alongside local signs. Watch what happens next. Divine love can find a way to point to something gloriously bigger and more. Even when it starts with something ordinary and small.

Get Practical

Start simple. Treat your altar or table (or entire chancel area) like a stage where the good news gets played out. If weekly plans are too much, try quarterly.

- First, craft the weekly worship guide from the Stone Soup chapter. It will coordinate and focus the worship work by clearly identifying the scripture, theme, and an anchoring image, sign, symbol, or question.

- Next, identify a big faith symbol—like the cross. It should be facing all worshipers. In a place where other signs or objects can be arranged to start a conversation about the weekly focus.

- Prayerfully ponder these two helpful questions: *How might worshipers engage the scripture with things that are personal or particular to your community? How could they use the stuff of their lives to encounter—not just think about—the good news?*

- Then, for curating clarity, write a short answer to these questions. Add it to the worship guide. For example, *Worshipers will explore Jesus' challenge not to worry (Luke 12:22-31) by bringing in signs of the things that worry them. For the call to prayer, they will place them in front of the altar. Then hear this reassuring scripture about God's care for even the lilies of the field.*

- Remember that objects placed at the altar or chancel area aren't simply ways for worshipers to interact with the scripture. They are also ways for the scripture to interact with them. We don't just interpret God's Word. It has a way of interpreting us right back.

- Objects can be added before or during worship. But be clear about the assignment. And how it fits with your order of worship. Is the action a call to worship? A response to the Word? Part of a confession or lament? A deepening of prayer? Name where it belongs.

- Place personal objects on the altar to represent those not physically present. Call attention to these signs at the gathering or during a time of prayer. This is an important way to include those worshiping virtually as well.

- When asking worshipers to bring a local sign, plan well in advance. Communicate the request clearly. Repeatedly. And with a sense of encouraging play- fulness: *Bring something that represents how you feel burdened or something that makes you hopeful.* Consider setting up a table with simple art supplies so "forgetters" can create their responses on the spot.

- Pay attention to the particulars of your community: the needs, aches, and celebrations. Include signs of them. For example: Load up the altar with the local harvest—stalks of corn, shocks of wheat, baskets of zucchini, and tomatoes.

- For curating clarity, identify how the signs connect to the salvation story. For example, Decorate the altar with fabrics from the refugee group moving into your community. *We will celebrate our new Congolese neighbors and remember our faith identity as those who welcome strangers (Leviticus 19:34).* Or, *The baskets of summer tomatoes will remind us that we can taste and see the goodness of the Lord. And share it with our neighbors.*

- If you start with the worship guide, trust that local signs and symbols can work well in silence. You don't have to add explanations. In fact, sometimes additional words merely dilute a holy moment. Increase the *interacting* among worshipers, ordinary objects, and holy symbols—not necessarily the *reporting* about it.

Start the Conversation

1. What faith symbols are included in your worship space? Choose one and try to describe all that it means. Are there still more descriptions?

2. Share a story of how a Christian symbol spoke to you without words.

3. As a group, name ten local signs—ordinary, familiar objects—that could start a worship conversation when placed in front of the cross. Describe one of these conversations.

4. Review Pastor Steve's story and the "Get Practical" section. What are the ideas that intrigue or delight you?

5. Make a plan to include local signs in worship. Note if this work feels awkward or uncertain. Then lovingly revisit this lesson after some experimenting, adapting, and learning. Has God been at work through local signs and symbols? Share what you've noticed.

Chapter Thirteen

Strength 5: Including Co-Creator Gifts
Seven Worship Strengths of Small Congregations

Maybe you've heard it said that excellent worship requires experts in areas like presenting, preaching, and singing. Maybe you've heard that other interests and hobbies really don't fit in worship. And unskilled folks need not apply.

But what if small congregations can work differently? They can include other talents and local interests as worship arts and offerings. The sacred seeks the company of the ordinary! So ordinary folks can be co-creators of worship with what they have and who they are.

Catch a Glimpse

Take note of the interests and talents of worshipers outside of Sunday mornings. List the hobbies and interests of those in your community. Things like baking, painting, motor maintenance, and home decorating. Then get creative. Imagine these as worship arts. Things that can be offered to God. Things that can reveal the

111

workings of divine love. Prayerfully curate your order of worship with these gifts. Give people and their interests a way to join the holy conversation.

Hear the Story

Alan was a longtime lay leader of two small congregations. He knew the community well. More importantly, he loved the community well. Alan had a knack for finding out what made someone light up. He paid attention and could list the interests, passions, activities, and hobbies of most community members.

In his congregations, Alan was also known for a mostly pleasant reminder: *Brothers and Sisters, worship is the work of the people. All the people. Not just the pastor!* This announcement was followed by passing out jobs: *Could you read the scripture? Lead the call to worship? Light the candles?*

But something had been bugging Alan for years. These Sunday morning jobs were a narrow slice of what these workers could do—what they *loved* to do. Their worship work had little connection to their rest-of-the-week passions and gifts. In fact, worship rarely included their very best gifts and interests.

Alan had seen Nancy's paintings. Most days, there was a paint smudge on her hands, shirt, or hair. She claimed it was just a "little hobby:" *Painting lets me think without words.* Alan noticed new canvases and clever color experiments every visit. *Delight!*

Alan had also witnessed Ross troubleshoot motors just by listening to them. He heard Ross's urgent reminders about properly maintaining equipment. *Craft!*

Alan had tasted the soups of Ruth, a local garden guru and pollinator protector: *Everyone needs nourishing food. And everyone needs bees!* Her harvests made the grocery store produce look puny. She couldn't walk up someone's driveway without pinching up certain weeds and leaving others. *Passion!*

Alan knew when the fourth graders would learn to play the recorder, starting with "When the Saints Go Marching In." And he cheered on the high school sports team in another losing season. He attended local dance and piano recitals. And genuinely appreciated young fingers taking on "Moonlight Sonata." Or new ballet shoes interpreting "You are my Sunshine." Not because any of the performances were perfect. But because they belonged to the whole community. *Connection!*

Alan also marveled when the regional quilters gathered in the community center. There was a hum of sewing machines. Chatter. And from scraps of fabric came gifts of warmth and striking works of art. *Transformation!*

He noted how Aaron made grocery displays at the Piggly Wiggly to celebrate local events. And how everyone stopped by to see his "Go Warthogs!" spelled out in paper towels. *Surprise!*

Alan loved chatting with Mason. The twelve-year-old was awkward around other children but could rival any geology professor when asked about his rock collection. Mason twinkled with information about each rock and mineral. *Wonder!*

And Alan smiled, seeing how Ben quietly saved wire from a brush pile behind the park to make cages for next spring's tomato plants. Already planning for a community garden. *Anticipation!*

So one week, Alan simply decided that these local gifts were, in fact, worship gifts.

After all, these were image-of-God people—*right?* Even when they didn't connect this precious identity to their rest-of-the-week activities.

It took considerable cajoling at first. No one thought that the thing they loved should be brought before God. Each thought it seemed like an ordinary weekday activity or interest. Not a special Sunday morning offering. But that was Alan's point. The Divine meets us in ordinary, everyday life. God was already showing up in gardens, garages, grade schools, and gravel pits. Seven days a week. The people just weren't recognizing it.

Alan was persistent, persuasive, and mostly pleasant.

Here's what happened. Alan reviewed the pastor's worship guide (the weekly scriptures and theme) ahead of time. Then, about once a month, he matched a theme with a local gift, hobby, or interest. He used his holy curiosity: *How could this thing—our thing—add to a conversation between God and the precious people right here? How could it be offered?* Nothing was fully scripted or rehearsed. It was more like adding a new dish to the potluck dinner.

Sometimes he would invite someone to set up a table in the chancel area and offer a gift, hobby, or interest *during worship.*

For instance, during the prelude, Nancy carried her caddy of supplies, an easel, and a big canvas into the sanctuary. While worshipers sang, prayed, and listened to a sermon on Psalm 23, she painted her experience of the scripture. The worshipers witnessed the paint strokes, drips, and color changes. Something new was happening: *Shadows of death, the light of goodness and mercy.* Together they *watched* reassurance, gratitude, and beauty emerge. Right there. At the final hymn, she placed it as an offering in front of the altar. On behalf of everyone. *Mystery.*

Alan knew the artwork would never be shown at the Louvre. Or even the county museum. But for years afterward, he noticed how worshipers referred to this experience: *Remember when we prayed with Nancy's painting? That's how the psalm feels to me now.* Or, *In the hospital, I kept thinking about how the dark purple and bright yellow went together.* Or, *Brother Alan, maybe I won't tell you no when you ask me to work in worship next time.*

So Alan kept asking. Periodically. Imaginatively. Lovingly. He matched up unexpected gifts and the good news. He called them "co-creator gifts." And made clear that they absolutely belonged in worship.

- Like when the pastor explored the importance of regular spiritual disciplines for the Christian life. And Ross methodically maintained and cleaned an old motor throughout the sermon. *Recognition!*

- Like when the theme was waiting on the Lord. And Ben bent and twisted wire to make tomato cages. And Ruth set up a gardener's table in front of the lectern. She planted tiny seeds in dozens of little clay pots. Layering drainage rock and potting soil. Adding kitchen compost. Watering. Tidying up the mess. Placing them along the altar rail. Quietly ready. *Anticipating.*

- Like when the quilters collected leftover cloth from worshipers. Then cut and pieced together a wildly colorful design right there in worship over the next few weeks. Unmatching flames! Just in time to be placed on the altar for Pentecost. *Unexpected beauty!*

Some were short co-creator moments.

- Like the benediction on All Saints Day. When a couple of fourth graders played "When the Saints Go Marching In" on their recorders. On the third verse, the congregation joined in with kazoos and danced out together. *Joy!*

- Or when the congregation finished a big food drive. Aaron surprised everyone by arranging the donations in front of the altar—Feed my sheep. He placed the bread and cup on top. *Communion!*

- Or when Mason enthusiastically laid out his ten all-time favorite rocks along the altar rails. He named them by category, classification, and special properties. His delight was infectious. With tears in her eyes, Mason's mom then led the congregation with a call to worship from Psalm 24: "The earth is the Lord's and all that is in it. . . ." *Awe!*

Everything worked somehow. Not because they were brilliant performances. But because they were genuine offerings. *Co-creator gifts.*

Alan knew that none of this would work in a big congregation. But he loved the people in this congregation and community. And knew God did too.

Connect the Dots

An important recap: worship is a mutual exchange between God and the gathered. We bring our best gifts. Whatever we have. From wherever we are. And the High Holy beyond us mysteriously meets us. To receive us and bless our gifts. To draw us closer.

But what qualifies as our "best gifts"? Well, the incarnational good news insists that it varies by the particulars of each community. By the ordinary stuff of each "right here" bunch of folks.

Skeptical?

Remember how Miriam celebrated God's rescue plan from Pharaoh by picking up a simple tambourine and busting out a poetry slam piece? No order of worship predicted it. Without other instruments or sheet music lying around, the other women danced together. Their bodies and movements were worship offerings. *Joy!*

Remember the ointment a woman scandalously slathered on Jesus' feet? Remember her tears? And the hair she used to wipe it all up because not even a decorative towel would be lavish enough? All worship gifts. Co-creator gifts. *Profound gratitude.*

Remember the fishes and loaves offered by that uppity kid who didn't grasp how puny his packed lunch really was? And what Jesus did with this gift anyway?

Christians have always celebrated worship with co-creator gifts. Worship has always been crafted from the ordinary stuff and familiar practices of imperfect people.

And here's the important part: God doesn't just tolerate this pattern until something better can be done.

God invites it! Just look at our sacraments. They are ordinary things transformed in an encounter with divine love. Bread becomes life. Wine is forgiveness. Water is cleansing and renewing. Gathered believers are the Church. Each gift is changed somehow in the offering. That's the point. Our best gifts offered to God—the ordinary stuff of each person and place—never stay ordinary. In worship, they become an encounter, a relationship, a holy exchange.

Bottom line: your worship should not be limited to a few recognized skill sets offered by a few good experts. Small congregations are exactly the places to explore beyond these limitations. But this exploration may require rethinking how you craft worship. Typically, in crafting worship, we think about these skills: planning and leading. But there's another essential, powerful skill for small congregations: *curating*.

Curating is the work of selecting, tending, organizing, and offering a collection—like a museum's collection, for example. The museum curator gathers items, preserves them, and ultimately displays groups of them for a particular purpose. To explore a particular theme: *See these pictures from the 1920s? Our town comes from hardworking immigrant families*. A curated collection helps tell a story. Or start a conversation. Or offer new insight. Or grow a community.

The same is true for worship. We curate. Our tradition has gifted us with an enormous collection of worship words and ways. We have music, scripture, sermons, sacred objects, and scholarship. Our tradition has also provided us with orders of worship. And themed seasons for offering the good news. Each week we *curate* worship from this precious collection. With help from lectionaries, hymnals, interpretive guides, and thematic worship series. We populate our orders of worship with our best gifts.

But we may be leaving out some meaningful, important gifts. Our collections are bigger than we could possibly imagine. Because they include not only the gifts of our tradition but also the gifts of our community. The local stuff. Like Alan noticed. From the actual places where we live and where God meets us.

Including these local gifts can shout the Gospel's message: *What you have is enough! Who you are is enough! The kingdom is among you! So lean in and listen! God knows what to do next.*

Time for a caveat. About the goal of all of this co-creating and collaborating in worship. Here it is: novelty is not the point. It's also not about spectacle. Or boundary-busting. Or proof of relevance. Co-creator gifts serve a much more important job than those things. These gifts should pull us into closer connection with the work of the Church. Most importantly, they should draw us deeper into the heart of God.

There's an essential and holy elegance at play. Gifts *from* God pull us back *to* God with gratitude. *Thanks, thanks, thanks to the Giver.*

By now, we can trust the pattern. All ordinary things can be transformed by divine love.

Get Practical

To curate worship with local co-creator gifts, start here.

- First, as always, start with the weekly worship guide: scripture, themes, images, signs, symbols, and questions. It should gently coordinate your work and help you curate local gifts.

- Next, act like Alan. Take up his spiritual practice: fall in love with your entire community. Notice what makes folks light up. See them with the eyes of Christ. Sometimes this takes prayerful work. Make sure you are drawing the circles of connection wide. Include lots of neighborhoods and demographics. Not just the ones you know. Curators need great love, great curiosity, and great connections.

- Keep a list of all the gifts, interests, talents, and hobbies around you. In both your congregation and community. Brainstorm and update regularly. Share them playfully. Nothing should be too big or too small. And remember not to screen out things that aren't the usual "churchy" things. Trust that God can bless and transform anything. Even our limited expectations.

- Include pastors and lay leaders in curating worship. Generally, the pastor should create the worship guide. Then work with a lay leader to imagine how a co-creator gift might be included. Start quarterly. With practice, consider a monthly co-creator gift. Remember that it takes faithful imagination. You don't need to rehearse, but you do need to collaborate.

- To avoid mere novelty or spectacle, prayerfully ponder these questions: *How does this gift help us explore or experience the good news? How does it deepen the focus of the Worship Guide?*

- Then, for curating clarity, write a short answer to these questions. Add it to the worship guide. For example, *As Mason shares the exquisite order and beauty of his rock collection, we will experience the psalmist's awe about our good Creator and the good creation.*

- Practice lavish hospitality with each co-creator. Recruit, encourage, appreciate, thank, repeat. This is an opportunity for you to know and love another person God already knows and loves. It's an opportunity to celebrate their created goodness, too.

- Review the lessons on "The Ikea Effect" (Chapter 7) and the "Happy Birthday Effect" (Chapter 5). Participation changes our experience. It can increase how we value something. So remember that co-creator gifts don't have to be fabulous stand-alone performances. They just need to be an offering. Shared among all of the gathered. For God.

- This strength will require experimenting, flailing, learning, adapting, and sharing. Like worship work always does.

Start a Conversation

1. Share a story of when you've offered something in worship. How did it affect you? Be specific. Does it continue to affect you?

2. Alan had a ministry gift, "a knack for finding out what made someone light up." Who has this gift in your congregation? How could you grow this as a spiritual practice in your congregation? List five places you could observe with love and curiosity this week. Then report back.

3. Share a story of when you had a gift or interest overlooked. Or when you were judged as not good enough. How did it affect you? Does it continue to affect you?

4. Make a hospitality plan for co-creators. How will you recruit, encourage, appreciate, and thank them? Be specific and lavish with this plan. How should the offerings of each person be received?

5. Start your list. See if you can name twenty-five local
    gifts, hobbies, interests, or talents. Remember, nothing
    is too big or small. Next, imagine how each might point
    us toward God. Ready to try for fifty?

Chapter Fourteen

Strength 6: Leading with Partnerships, Not Proprietorships

Seven Worship Strengths of Small Congregations

Maybe you've heard it said that congregations require a clear identity and focused direction. They need a brand of worship and ministry linked to the church's name. So pastors should lead top-down and find the best one-size-fits-most programs for their settings. Then invite laity to chase all the resources these programs will require (sigh).

But what if leadership can work differently in small settings—with a messy web of partnerships? Clergy can team up with laity. Both can team up with community organizations—even other congregations. In groups and as individuals. So the church can work across the boundaries of organization types, denominations, and official ownership.

Because Christianity is not a brand. And the kingdom of God is not proprietary.

Catch a Glimpse

Quit looking for that one "right" program or that one "right" pastor. That kind of "this is ours" program-thinking tends to paralyze small congregations. Instead, seek partnerships. All kinds. Between clergy and laity. But also in your community with individuals, organizations, and even other congregations. Partner up one by one and in groups. Start a list with the particular needs and gifts already present among all of you. Work from the bottom up. Then faithfully wager: *I bet there's a way.* . . .

Oh, yes, and celebrate all of these partnerships each week in worship.

Hear the Story

Sandy had learned to work with lots of different pastors. She had to. Over eighteen years, twelve pastors had served her small congregation. Some were full-time. Some were bi-vocational. Some were shared with a nearby congregation. A couple of the pastors stayed for three years. Several of them moved to larger settings in their first year. One left ministry entirely within a few months. There were also a few seasons with an interim pastor or a rotation of lay leaders. So Sandy had seen many leadership styles.

Sandy also worked as an assistant manager at a regional bank. The bank was well-regarded across several counties. Everyone recognized their brand and their way of doing business. She valued the professional, corporate leadership. The organization was program-driven. Efficient. Responsive to the big community needs. It worked with a clear, top-down vision that kept everyone on the same page. And provided the ideal resources for each set of tasks.

But Sandy noticed that many of her bank's corporate practices didn't seem to work at her small congregation:

God knows we've tried. The pastoral leadership was too inconsistent. There never seemed to be a program that fit. The members resisted top-down visions. They wanted to be heard more than they wanted to be efficient. And, well, it always felt like there were never *enough* resources— much less *ideal* resources. For anything.

Sandy cringed, remembering the pastor who had served a large congregation during seminary. He came in with corporate confidence. A clear vision of powerful worship: *I know this works!* He provided a detailed list of what they would need: new music, better technology, and a different *brand.* The congregation was cautiously hopeful: *Is this the fix we need?*

But then resistance crept in. It was fueled by an unspoken mix of fear and shame. This pastor's vision left little room for the usual worship workers. They weren't partners. So they quietly stepped back, feeling as if they had been fired. The pastor was chasing a performative worship style everyone knew was drawing big crowds a few miles away. But he was frustrated about the lack of quality local musicians: *A great drummer is essential!* And it all felt awkward somehow among sixty people. He tried a worship design team. They met weekly— *diligently*—for a few months. Then burned out.

By the second year, both he and the congregation felt disillusioned. Damaged: *Maybe we are just not enough.*

Sandy recognized that this pastor and the congregation were chasing a program. A settled, systems answer. A specific thing that could fix them. In addition, they wanted a *proprietorship.* Something that would be "theirs." Something with a recognized, distinctive brand.

But the chasing wasn't working. There didn't seem to be enough: *Was it not enough vision? Or resources? Or . . . worth?*

She also remembered a handful of other pastors—ones who seemed to bring abundant resources with them. Each was talented in music, preaching, teaching, working with technology. Even decorating the altar. So they ended up doing everything themselves. Because, truthfully, they did everything well. Better than anyone else could.

But this turned the pastor into the program. Or, more accurately, it created a sole proprietorship. The pastor's brand became the congregation's brand. And it didn't last. These pastors were eventually moved. And they left the congregation a little smaller and more hesitant without them.

Not enough—again.

Occasionally denominational leaders came in to help. The message was named gently but painfully: *Maybe you're just not equipped for this work. Congregational hospice is an option.*

But Sandy knew that *community* hospice was not. This congregation was tasked to build the kingdom of God right where they were. With whatever they had. They were there to love these neighbors—people who might otherwise be overlooked.

Sandy heard the worshipers' worries: *We don't have enough kids for a children's program. There aren't enough musicians for a praise band. Our food pantry is pitifully small compared to the one by the post office.* But she also heard the quiet question behind these worries: *So who are we?*

One evening, a pang of recognition hit her while filling out some denominational paperwork. The documents were all about proving their identity with proprietary programs. The stuff they "owned:" like their kids' ministries, their community outreach, their small groups. The kinds of things that could be branded, controlled, and recognized: *Brought to you by First Church.* Or, *Brought to you by Pastor Mark.*

But these kinds of things had not worked.

She took on the familiar words of faithful prophets: *It doesn't have to be this way.* But what was the alternative?

She found it hiding in plain sight. Among the laity. Sandy began to notice partnerships. Not congregational ownerships. But worshiper collaborations. Just faithful folks working with each other. With their community. Even with other congregations. They worked in pairs, small groups, and as individuals. They worked not according to a single, top-down, coordinated corporate plan. But in a loose network of bottom-up partners instead: *Here's what I have. Maybe it can help?*

Like Margaret, for example, who was already volunteering at the big food pantry. She led its expansion to include undocumented workers in the area. Then she put these workers on an advisory board. *Maybe our church doesn't need its own pantry. Maybe it just needs to better help with this established work. As a partner. We don't need recognition. We need full bellies and neighbors with dignity.*

Sandy asked Margaret to stack her weekly haul of groceries and diapers in front of the altar each Sunday before taking them downtown. In worship, Margaret shared the stories of this partnership. What she saw. What she learned. How the relationships changed her. The haul grew.

The congregation switched their communion bread

and juice to whatever was offered that week at the big pantry. It was not just a partnership. It was *communion.*

There was also Shawn, who worked unofficially as a job counselor. He had retired as a school resource officer. But he still knew all the helpful people and programs in the region. Everyone in the community agreed there was a need for work mentors and apprenticeships. But no one had enough resources for such an ambitious program. Shawn thought perhaps he could work with other congregations in the area. And maybe include the local trade union? And those contractors eager for skilled labor?[31] *Maybe in the kingdom of God, we are like the yeast!*[32]

Then there was Alma, the pianist. She just happened to be best friends with musicians at four churches. They served in different denominations. But they shared the same passion for God—and for teaching others how to make a joyful noise. *What if they collaborated—not just cooperated? What if they created something new together?* The five friends imagined offering a shared summer music camp for kids in the apartment complex on the other side of town. The ones often referred to as *"those* kids." No one knew if it would work.

More importantly, no one needed to own it exclusively. The musicians could be creative risk-takers *together.* They recruited two high school choir students who lived in the complex. They treated them as valued partners. In return, the girls taught them that *"those* kids" were our kids. All of ours.

---

[31] Thanks to the inspiration and work of Allen T. Stanton, *Reclaiming Rural: Building Thriving Rural Congregations* (New York: Roman & Littlefield, 2021).

[32] Matthew 13:31-33.

Sandy clearly saw the partnership possibilities. And she saw the difference between exploring a messy webs of mutual relationships and insisting on a tidy congregation-owned program. So she helped her congregation create two lists:

- **List 1 included individual needs in the whole community.**

  o The shelter needs someone to do yard work and laundry.

  o The Lewis twins need to matter to someone.

  o The school reports more hungry kids and families.

- **List 2 gathered all the gifts, talents, and interests already among them—in both the congregation and the community.**

  o Who could help set up a trade school?

  o Hey, don't the twins play guitar?

  o Mark is off work on Fridays and has a weed whacker.

  o Patti always knows the coolest toys and activities for children.

The lists got longer over the months.

Sandy reminded new pastors that the congregation wanted to partner with them, too. The congregation might not have exclusive programs. They might not have ideal resources. But they could work with others. They could step across proprietary "these are mine" boundaries and serve. Anywhere. With anyone. For small settings, partnerships make good sense. They also make good-news sense. The Church's work is always all-in with all creation. And God's kingdom always exceeds our branding anyway.

In worship, the congregation began lighting a candle for each partnership. They started praying for each person, each mission, and each kingdom possibility. Their weekday work was routed through their Sunday work. Worship reinterpreted the tasks done together. Over time, folks quit worrying: *Who are we?* Instead, they just celebrated: *Brought to you by a bunch of neighbors who love Jesus. Want to join in?*

Some did. And here's the intriguing part. The congregation started embracing new leadership practices. They were practices that probably wouldn't show up at Sandy's bank. But they were practices that worked in a small congregation—*wonderfully, surprisingly.*

The first new leadership practice was wagering: *I bet there's a way.* They quit starting meetings with a plan of how things ought to work. With resources they didn't have. Instead, they started with this hopeful, messy invitation: *I wonder if we could . . . ? What do you think? God can make do. We can, too.* They read aloud the two lists that Sandy had started. Then added in lots of faithful, curious conversations with their neighbors: *I'd wager there's someone who could help us with this work. Maybe **we** can join in **their** work.*

The second new leadership practice was "lone lamb chasing." They realized they had quit looking for lambs—for each one who needed care. Instead, they had been anxiously waiting for a fully developed flock management system. Or a single wrangler they could hire to handle the work expertly. But ministry didn't require a critical mass of needs and resources. Or another sole

132

proprietorship. They could have a Lewis twins ministry without waiting for a youth ministry. They could *be* youth ministers without *having* a youth minister. So they started treating all lay members as lay leaders. Because, of course, they are.

Perhaps some of the "lone lamb care" would result in a flock. Someday. Or maybe not. But in the meantime, it was a holy, scripture-approved way to engage the world. It was the unreasonable, each-one inefficiency of grace.

Together these two practices managed to end their program-thinking paralysis. They quit waiting on a single leader, a clear vision, the right stuff, and their own brand.

To be clear, not every partnership worked. But the congregation learned that small places could be magnificently nimble. The church realized it could make changes in a few weeks that would take Sandy's bank a whole season and thousands of emails. *Maybe that's why the kingdom is like a bunch of tiny mustard seeds.*[33] *Not a grove of replanted sequoias.*

Two years after Sandy started the lists, there was more participation. Seldom-attending members showed up again: *Well, I heard you might know who needs a side of beef.* Folks from other congregations and the community dropped by: *Can our divorce recovery group meet here while the roof gets fixed?*

And the congregation began to entertain some ridiculous, unexpected new ideas: *There's not enough affordable housing for students at the community college.*

---

[33] Matthew 17:20.

You have several acres close by. Could you imagine a new kind of partnership? [34]

Holy possibilities. Partnerships—not proprietorships: *Brought to you by the kingdom of God already among us.*

Connect the Dots

The possibility of this strength showed up in some conversations with groups of retiring clergy from large congregations. Leaving ministry, these pastors were all looking forward to attending worship and programs in *other* congregations. And joining in *other* community events. Not their own.

There had been invisible boundaries in their ministries. There were unspoken, unnamed expectations about their leadership roles. The denomination had not laid out these boundaries. No one learned them in seminary. But nearly all felt them. And kept them. Sometimes uncomfortably.

So what were these invisible boundaries?

These pastors knew to participate almost exclusively in their *own* congregation's work. To support it. And, perhaps more importantly, to *represent* it. They felt a responsibility to maintain a certain brand of ministry and worship. And the brands of these big settings were not messy webs of mutual partners. Their brands were specific, recognizable ministry programs and worship. *Property?* They were the kinds of things that belonged to one congregation. Theirs. And all work was routed and coordinated through their leadership. Big settings simply

---

[34] See http://rootedgood.org. And yes, you need to read this: Mark Elsdon, *We Aren't Broke: Uncovering Hidden Resources for Mission and Ministry* (Grand Rapids: William B. Eerdmans Publishing Company, 2021). Now.

have to work that way—*right?*

But small ones don't. And maybe there is a freedom in small congregations that these retiring pastors longed for. Their discomfort with keeping these boundaries may be telling. Perhaps the boundaries served a *practical* rather than *theological* function.

And maybe, for the love of God, it doesn't *have* to be this way.

Let's start with some rough definitions painted with a broad brush. A *proprietorship* is simply a way of establishing an ownership relationship. That's why it shares a root word with *proprietary. Property.* It indicates there's some kind of fixed thing. And someone (or some institution) owns it. Exclusively. And hence, wants to protect it. And decide what happens next with this fixed thing.

Partnerships, however, can be looser, messier beasts. With webs of connections. They usually get called in for shared endeavors. Collaborations. Sometimes the collaborators are equal partners. Sometimes not. Sometimes there is a big bunch of co-creators. Sometimes just a few. Sometimes the endeavor is a fixed, defined thing. But often, it's a changing thing. With the addition of each new partner, the work, vision, and resources can change. Often unpredictably. Partnerships can be wildly creative. Innovative. Unexpected. Like that incident of a chocolate bar bumping into a jar of peanut butter. Or the venture of a small church leaping into student housing.

Practically, it's easy to understand how large congregations might work like proprietorships. Their distinctive work—ministry and worship—is a kind of valuable property. Their branding is a way to be recognized and invite more people in. But then there's that awkward question: *Is the brand **this** church, **The Church**, or the whole kingdom of God?*

The answer can quietly limit possibilities. Like those invisible boundaries corralling the retiring clergy. If the brand is *this* church, it may be easy to overlook partners. If the brand is *our* program/ministry/identity, we may not recognize other kingdom-of-God collaborators among us. Or the kingdom itself.

Maybe this is why scripture keeps hammering on that theme of unlikely partners. The ragtag bunch of enslaved "nobodies" from Egypt. Those unpolished fishers-turned-disciples. And, yes, every last one of us.

The divine mission is not something done *to* us but *with* us. Ministry always works best that way. *With*, not *to*. So the people we serve become precious collaborators too. It all sounds like a partnership, right?

Maybe the incarnation itself works more like a messy partnership than a proprietorship. Through Jesus, God shares a holy endeavor with us: *The Church!* This means the divine rescue plan is a partnership! With ever-changing, ever-adding collaborators. And a mission that reaches out like a web and can't be reduced to just one official program. The good news insists on the worth of all those collaborators. Each one. Every last one. The Holy Spirit knows how to make do with whatever they have. Divine love graciously partners up with imperfect people and uncertain plans. *Thank God!*

So maybe, for small congregations, it's time to stop

seeking a single clear vision. With one "right" program or leader. Maybe it's time to join in messy, unlikely partnership webs instead. Maybe it's time to step over our invisible boundaries. We can bet that the kingdom is bigger than our expectations. And it's waiting to be recognized already among us.

Get Practical

The starting place for this work is Sandy's set of lists.

- First, as a group, create List 1. Keep and regularly review particular needs in your community. Not just little ones. And not just big ones that call for more than your congregation could ever possibly do. List all of them. Pray for insight into the work of your congregation. And the whole Church.

- Then, create List 2 together. Develop a list of gifts, interests, talents, and resources *already set in motion around your community*. Pay attention to potential partners. Meet for coffee with neighbors and organizations. Learn about what other groups, service providers, individuals, and congregations are doing. And what they need.

- Make ministry participation expectations bigger in your congregation. Are members serving only your congregation's projects and programs? Invite them to reach further. To serve the community, find partnerships, and step across the dividing lines of "ownership."

- Celebrate the partners and partnerships in worship. Every week. Tell the local ministry stories that reveal the good news at work. Or the stories that nudge us to work. Testify to how the partnerships have changed *you*. Not just how you have changed those served.

- Create a culture of partnerships—one where they are not just permitted but sought and encouraged. Specifically, seek ways to work with other congregations. Small churches are often clustered in small communities. And often, those communities have big needs— ones that will require you to step over invisible boundaries—like denomination. Where do you need to start growing relationships and building partnerships to serve your community? Remember, Christianity is not a brand to be protected.

- Be attentive to the patterns of toxic charity or colonialism.[35] These tend to show up when one party is always the giver. And another is always the receiver. This pattern can lock in unjust patterns rather than reimagine them. It can turn precious children into "those kids." Somehow find ways to treat all parties as partners. Insist on mutual relationships. Where all participants can create something together. And where receivers can also add their gifts to List 2. Like the families on Margaret's advisory board. Or the congregation's communion celebration that shared food pantry goods. Or those high school students who helped guide the summer music camp. *Mutuality is usually a feature of successful partnerships. And always a feature of the kingdom of God.*

---

[35] See, for example, Robert D. Lupton, *Toxic Charity: How Churches and Charities Hurt Those They Help (and How to Reverse It)* (San Francisco: HarperOne, 2011).

Start the Conversation

1. Has your congregation been anxiously looking for that one "right" program or leader? Tell the story together. Ask the Spirit to give you new ministry glasses.

2. Compassionately tell the story of your congregation's leadership—laity and clergy. What kinds of leadership styles have you experienced? What kinds of things worked (or didn't)?

3. Humbly review any patterns of resistance with leaders in your congregation. Resistance may be spoken and obvious. Or quietly subversive. Listen carefully for the message behind it. Do fear or shame play a role in the resistance? How might the good news talk back?

   Bonus: Prayerfully discern if you need to seek forgiveness from a leader. Then do it.

4. Describe the roles of lay leaders in your congregations. Would you describe your congregation as lay-led? Why or why not? How could laity take on fuller partnership roles in worship and ministry?

5. Start your List 1 and List 2 together. Return to them often. Grow them. Share them. Pray through them. See the world with them. Repeat. Repeat. Repeat. What do you notice?

Chapter Fifteen

Strength 7: Widening the Word
Seven Worship Strengths of Small Congregations

Maybe you've heard it said that sermons should be twenty-minute, climax-of-worship, powerfully-delivered monologues by an expert.

But what if small congregations can widen how the Word is proclaimed? Sermons can gather folks around a table instead of a pulpit. They can proclaim the good news in a variety of collaborative forms—questions, meditations, dialogues, testimonies, and other arts. And they can be led and shaped by different kinds of faithful folks—both pastors and laity.

Catch a Glimpse

Plan quarterly to include additional forms of proclamation in place of the usual sermon. This doesn't mean bringing in a guest preacher. It means imagining new ways to encounter the Word of God. Like gathering worshipers around a table to share stories related to a scripture. Or gathering the testimony of two or three laity on a shared theme. Or asking questions about a scripture together (without feeling pressure to answer them all). Or letting the congregation listen in on a conversation among faith leaders in your community. Or inviting worshipers to share a symbol and a short statement of when God has shown up for them. Or . . . well, see how you can widen the offering of the Word for your congregation.

Hear the Story

Pastor Heidi returned from a large denominational gathering. It felt good to eat, visit, worship, and learn with hundreds of other faithful folks. The sermons were compelling and inspirational. The workshops were helpful. *Mostly.* As usual, she returned home with several new books to place alongside the other new books from the last meeting (some still unread). There was a familiar pang looking at the shelf. She felt a heaviness: *These are things we should be doing well. But aren't.*

In the quiet of her office behind the sanctuary, she decided to listen deeply to this heaviness. *Prayerfully.* And she noticed three contradictory thoughts poking her all at once. *Come Holy Spirit, I need your help to sort this out.*

- **Poke 1:** She felt an unspoken judgment that her small congregation (and all the other small ones) were not measuring up somehow. She worried that her preaching was not powerful. It certainly didn't soar like those beautifully crafted center-piece proclamations from the big gathering. *Maybe I'm what's not measuring up.*

- **Poke 2:** She recognized that much of what worked at the big gathering wouldn't work in her congregation. It was the quiet truth known by all small-setting pastors. Worship resources can't be dragged and dropped from big settings into small ones. They risk sounding awkward. Or pretentious. Like they don't fit. Maybe her denomination just needed workshops on how to dial down great worship. So it fits small settings. *But wait, the good news can't be dialed down, right?*

- **Poke 3:** She remembered starting ministry. The very idea of preaching intimidated her: *I don't know all the answers, much less how to proclaim them!* A beloved seminary professor offered reassurance, "God can do more with questions than answers. Ask them." She knew sermons are never stand-alone performances. They are always just a part of the whole worship conversation between God and *all* the people: *So how can I invite my congregation into this work?*

The Spirit invited a playful response to all three of these pokes. She kept listening. And began experimenting. With measuring worship differently. Not dialing it down. And widening the ways that the Word was offered in her congregation's worship.

One Sunday, she invited two retired pastors from other denominations to participate in the service. Instead of the usual sermon, the three pastors simply talked together about Luke 10—the passage where a religious scholar tests Jesus with a question. Jesus winds up defining "neighbor" in a way that everyone agreed with. But also disagreed with.

Not a surprise: all three pastors heard the story a little differently. Big surprise: the worshipers recognized that God's Word is wide enough for differences. "Wide

Word Sundays" became a quarterly celebration. They led to sharing additional worship events with other congregations. *Imagine that.*

On another Sunday, Heidi invited three lay leaders to share a short testimony. She planned and recruited well in advance. The scripture that day told the story of how Abraham and Sarah were changed by offering lavish hospitality to strangers. She asked each lay leader to share a story of being changed by serving someone.

On one potluck Sunday, Pastor Heidi moved worship to the fellowship hall. And, yes, there was complaining at first. Each table had large-print copies of Acts 2:43-47, a story of life among the early believers. Each copy also included this prompt: *When have you experienced a meal with glad and generous hearts? Offer your story.* In place of the sermon, there was deep sharing. And deep listening. She noticed that both guests and regulars participated fully. As if worship truly was the work of *all* the people. Pastor Heidi smiled when they complained about ending early. Because they were actually ending thirty minutes late.

For one Thanksgiving Sunday, the congregation had just cleaned up from serving a meal to the whole community. The servers were all weary. Many worried about the cost of a new roof that looked unavoidable. *Do we have enough?* She asked them to bring an object that reminded them of their gratitude to God. They read a psalm of thanksgiving. In place of the usual sermon, each worshiper placed an object on the altar. And each offered a sentence or two explanation. The congregation responded to each: *God is so good. With love that never runs out.* The altar became crowded with signs of provision and care. All packed in around the bread and cup. The experience was the Word proclaimed: *Yes, and more than enough.*

Occasionally, Pastor Heidi took a leap from the security of her sermon manuscript and simply shared her questions about the scripture. Or invited the worshipers' questions. She noticed that folks pondered these questions long after worship. Her visits to the grocery store often included sermon follow-ups: *Hey, Pastor Heidi, that scripture got me wondering . . .*

One week, a local potter set up a wheel in the chancel area. They read Jeremiah 18. Then they meditated while watching the potter prepare the clay and shape a pitcher. The work took several tries. Afterwards, worshipers shared their reflections—on centering, shaping, messing up, starting over, and being reshaped. *Can't the Lord do the same with us?*

Another week Pastor Heidi assigned worshipers to different characters in the story of the Prodigal Son. They unpacked the reasonableness of each character. And the foolishness of the father whose love could not be contained by reason. *Oh, yes, that's grace.*

Over time—and more books on her office shelf—Pastor Heidi learned how to better guide a conversation for the sermon. Not a lecture. But a holy, sometimes messy engagement *with* the people. She started with her planned weekly focus and prayerful study. But the tricky part was trying to avoid tidying everything up. Or making her voice the final authority.

She recognized that people seemed most affected by some of the unsettled moments of well-considered plans. Like when a visiting child heard the story of the Prodigal

Son. The boy breathlessly gasped at how great it would be to have a father who eagerly waited for him. And even planned a party with lots of food! *Indeed!*

In another unsettled moment, Pastor Heidi was exploring a psalm of lament with the congregation. She explained that the psalms make one thing perfectly clear: We are not limited to bringing our "joys and concerns" to God. We can bring our "joys and agonies." *What have we been silencing unnecessarily?*

One man who had lost a child years earlier spoke his pain. It was raw, uncomfortable, and honest. The kind of thing God longs to hear in worship but usually doesn't. Heidi allowed his emotion to fill the sanctuary. *Silence.* Then the oldest member of the congregation spoke slowly: "I'm just so sorry. I know I can cry to God. But sometimes there are no words. So I just take the next breath and let the Spirit sigh through me. Maybe we can breathe with you." Not another word was spoken for several minutes. They breathed, and wept, and sighed together. Then gathered around the table to continue this mystery of communion with the bread and cup.

Heidi realized that none of these holy encounters would likely happen at a big worship gathering. The unscripted, unsettled stuff in her congregation was too unpredictable. They required a different kind of planning and presence. But these intimate encounters were an extraordinary gift for her congregation. And perhaps for the whole Church. Because *all* those kinds of preaching encounters—with questions, arts, conversations, testimony, and even silence—show how far God will go to be with us.

The heart of God has never been a narrow thing to proclaim!

Connect the Dots

First, this essential acknowledgment. This short chapter does not qualify as a study of homiletics. It cannot substitute for the variety of excellent preaching resources available. Or provide a small-congregation detour around proclaiming the Word of God lavishly and well every week.

Instead, this chapter offers a narrow and simple strength for small settings. Here it is. *Small congregations have more options for proclaiming the Word than large ones.*

To grasp this strength, remember some of the practical concerns of big settings. Large congregations require predictability to coordinate crowds of people. And to repeat everything at 10:30 and 12:00. The work requires a settled script. And the script typically includes one recognized preacher. Not because God says so but because it's a valuable part of their identifying brand. Large churches also have to anticipate a wide variety of folks. So an easily recognizable, consistent format is helpful.

But none of these concerns should limit small congregations. Neither practically nor theologically.

Yes, there's an elephant in the narthex. So let's name it. Denominational leaders frequently criticize small-congregation preaching. Preaching is an anxious topic for many pastors. And the critique of worship often gets reduced to the quality of the sermon. Plus, sometimes worshipers complain about *sermons* because it's easier than finding words for that overwhelming, wordless *fear of decline.*

The simple comparison of sermons between small and large settings is also problematic. The preachers' job descriptions are not equivalent. Large congregations come with additional professional resources and focused responsibilities. Small congregations come with expectations that the pastor will be a jack-of-all-trades. With a staff-of-one. Today there's a general fear that small-congregation sermons aren't measuring up. But maybe it's time to measure *out* instead.

The Christian tradition provides a wealth of things to explore. We are gifted with wide ways to proclaim the Word of God! Small congregations have permission to work differently. They also have the blessing of great teachers and companions along the way.

The term *homily* simply means interaction. And *sermon* literally just means "talk." Nothing fancier than that. In the call-and-response pattern of Christian worship, there are many ways to interact and talk. There are loads of different kinds of conversations, including ones rooted in the strengths of small settings!

Mike Graves, a professor of preaching and worship, reminds us that before there were pulpit proclamations *to* worshipers, there were table conversations *with* them. And even these table conversations included a great variety of patterns. There were voted-on topics for discussion, art expressions, professional speakers. And plenty of participation.[36]

Historian of Christian worship Lester Ruth reminds us that the Early Church leaned away from fully scripted worship. It favored a format that embraced "an open-endedness of time."[37] Eucharistic prayers were created

---

[36] Mike Graves, *Table Talk: Rethinking Communion and Community* (Eugene, OR: Cascade Books, 2017).

[37] Lester Ruth, *Flow: The Ancient Way to Do Contemporary Worship* (Nashville: Abingdon Press, 2020).

in real-time. These worshipers recognized a need to respond and adjust in the moment. To avoid missing unexpected work of the Spirit. They weren't trying to create something repeatable.

Reread some of Paul's writing. You'll notice that he communicated differently depending on the audience. Christian "talk" always takes on particular communities. In their vernacular. Sermons can't be universal or uniform. Each sermon talks to-with-for a specific group of folks. Right where they are. And as they are. Like those Corinthians (*bless their hearts*) or the Galatians (*sigh*).

The Church keeps relearning that skill of Paul. That preaching requires unpacking[38] each scripture. *And* that preaching also requires unpacking each *community*. It seeks the stories, challenges, and forms that fit *these* people. So the good news can take on their flesh, too.

We have never needed to come up with a this-will-preach-anywhere sermon. And small settings have never needed to proclaim the Word of God in a way that makes sense to a tri-state area. Or that shows up in a generally recognized style. As Leonora Tubbes Tisdale names it, preaching can be "Local Theology and Folk Art."[39] *Yes, the incarnational monkey wrench again.*

This very recognition about preaching comes with some intriguing good-news consequences. It means we can include more forms and possibilities. More voices. More proclamation partners. Clergy *and* laity!

---

[38] Fancy word: exegeting. With thanks to Fred Craddock, *Preaching* (Nashville: Abingdon Press, 1985).

[39] Leonora Tubbs Tisdale, *Preaching as Local Theology and Folk Art* (Minneapolis: Fortress Press, 1997).

So we aren't surprised when Anna Carter Florence reminds us that preaching can be testimony.[40] And that testimony is not just an ancient form of sharing faith. It also comes with bonus features that we should celebrate now. Testimony is always contextual. And deeply participatory.

But there's more. Testimony has a history of being most vibrant in marginalized communities. *Like the good news often is!* Even while the Church has officially and painfully excluded certain folks from preaching, testimony was running a kind of Underground Railroad of proclamation. It included more bodies, voices, stories, and experiences: *Here's what I know about God; make of it what you will.*[41]

So preaching as testimony not only *expresses* the good news, it also *embodies* it. In unexpected places. Corners and edges. The very spots where Phyllis Tickle says the reach of the Church keeps widening. *Somehow.* Despite our anxious, irritable rummage sales.[42] *Thank God!*

Yes, this chapter comes with lists of books. But these books are priceless treasures, not judgments. Small congregations can take heart! Your sister in Christ, Lucy Rose, can guide you in *Preaching in the Roundtable Church*.[43] Your brother, Mike Graves, can help you imagine lively "table talk" for your community.[44] Your faith friend and scholar, Casey T. Sigmond, can help you

---

[40] Anna Carter Florence, *Preaching as Testimony* (Louisville: Westminster John Knox Press, 2007).

[41] Florence, *Preaching*.

[42] See Chapter 1. Phyllis Tickle, *The Great Emergence: How Christianity is Changing and Why* (Grand Rapids: Baker Books, 2008).

[43] Lucy Atkinson Rose, *Sharing the Word: Preaching in the Roundtable Church* (Louisville: Westminster John Knox Press, 1997).

[44] See Mike Graves, *Table Talk*.

prep and proclaim with "conversation and relationality."[45] In ways that honor real questions. Not just easy answers.

The variety of preaching models and forms should delight us—not overwhelm us. Because we have wide ways to offer the Word. And an abundance of faithful partners. Small congregations don't have to go it alone. Or seek special *permission*. They should recognize their invitation to explore. To reclaim, learn, imagine, partner up, embody, and translate the good news.

Start by practicing conversational sermons with your worshipers. In this time of enormous change and challenge, perhaps it's not helpful to insist on preaching in a way that ends discussions, silences debates. Or asserts the authority of a single expert. God can work with our questions and questioning. *Alleluia!*

Still overwhelmed? Try one of these options:

- **Put the conversation part *before* the sermon**. For instance, ask: *What emotions does this scripture prompt in you?* Or, *Be still for a moment and then share a word or phrase in this scripture that speaks to you.* You could ask, *What big, honest question do you have about this passage? Any little, seemingly petty ones? God's not afraid of either, but I am sometimes.*

- **You can also invite conversation *during* the sermon**. By sharing your vulnerable questions and interactions with a scripture: *Sometimes I worry that I'm so committed to being realistic that I might not have recognized resurrected Jesus either.*

---

[45] Casey T. Sigmon, "Preaching in the Process Theological Family," *Preaching the Manifold Grace of God: Theologies of Preaching in the Early Twenty-First Century*, (Eugene, OR: Cascade Books, 2022), 274-290.

It wouldn't compute! Then prepare requests for worshipers' responses and questions: *Why do you think our tradition keeps routing us through this quiet Easter story? What feels true about it? Where else have we seen God work with surprise? I wonder why?*

- **Or call for conversation *after* the sermon.** By inviting responses to a prepared, generous question like, *Where has the Spirit nudged you today in worship?* Or, *What words would you like to whisper in Mary's ear as she enters the garden on Easter morning? Could you whisper them for us, too?*

Look for ways to include laity and testimony. Not with an impoverished invitation of whatever-you-want-to-say or anything-goes. But with a lavish request: *Here's a scripture and theme. Can you share what you know, what you've experienced?* So the sermon and the rest of the service work together. And everyone can worship together.

Periodically, prayerfully craft a proclamation form that allows *all* the people to preach. Like Heidi's Thanksgiving proclamation: *What represents your gratitude to God? Explain in a sentence or two.*

From time to time, find a way to get out of pews. And around tables. Move worship from the sanctuary to the fellowship hall. Prayerfully prepare prompts for worshipers. So they can connect the scripture story to their own stories. Faithfully imagine the best ways for each person to share.

Trust the abundance in all of these proclamations. Perhaps this abundance will reassure the Church that digital worship also comes in many different forms for different communities. And with different strengths for small settings. Because we've not yet hit limits on how wide God's Word is willing to reach. *Of course.*

So preach, small congregations. Explore lavishly. Courageously. With "faith-full" variety. Right where you are. As if you are called to bring the good news to every last place on Earth. You are.

Get Practical

Another critical caveat: "Widening the Word" does not mean *less* preparation. It means *different* preparation. The usual sermon study and writing are replaced with careful curating—not a week off.

- Start by crafting the weekly worship guide from the Stone Soup chapter: scripture, theme, anchoring image, sign, symbol, or question. The guide will coordinate and focus the worship. Not in a rigid, fully-scripted way. But in a flexible, invitational way. So everyone can collaborate with their best gifts.

- Start small when widening the proclamation of the Word. Maybe once a month—or even once a quarter. Imagine how to include other formats, patterns, and voices. Which examples from Pastor Heidi delighted you somehow?

- Plan for a conversational sermon in one of the formats listed above. With interaction before, during, or after the usual sermon. Don't try to wing it. These will likely take *more* time to study and plan initially.

- Write out, revise, and practice any questions you might ask. Care in crafting worship is one of those lavish gifts we offer God.

- Move back to the fellowship hall. Plan worship that gathers folks around tables to share their stories—*in response to a specific scripture and prompt.* Consider sending the prompt in advance to anyone who cannot attend in person. Let them write or record their proclamation story. Anticipate both pushback and delight.

- Explain the possibilities and challenges of this strength to your congregation. Invite them to be partners. To explore together how to widen the Word. Ask for their feedback, encouragement, ideas, and prayerful support.

- Remember that a performance aesthetic will signal worshipers to expect polished expertise. A participation aesthetic will invite others to help figure it out. Recall the power of "The IKEA Effect" and the "Happy Birthday Effect."[46] We experience something differently—and more generously—when we help create it.

- Search out intergenerational worship resources. Generally, if things work better for children, they work better for everyone. Attention to the needs of children (and differently-abled persons) will suggest new ways of widening the Word. Check out the Messy Church movement,[47] for example.

- Feeling anxious about this strength? None of this requires throwing out trusted, familiar tools and traditions. You'll just be adding some new ones. Or maybe resurrecting some really old ones.

---

[46] See Chapter 7 for "The IKEA Effect" and Chapter 5 for the "Happy Birthday Effect."

[47] https://messychurchusa.org.

Start the Conversation

1. What are your congregation's practices for proclaiming the Word of God? Name them in detail. Who preaches? For how long? Where does it fit in worship? What are the kinds of formats? How does your congregation support your pastor's sermon and worship preparation?

2. Look back over all the ways Pastor Heidi explored and reclaimed sermons. Share honestly with each other. Which ones delighted you? Which ones made you nervous? Dig into why. Then listen for the Spirit's compassion and challenge.

3. Name one practice of "Widening the Word" you would like to try. Imagine it together— playfully, lovingly. Share, *What if we . . . ?*

4. Make a list of any hidden challenges for hearing the Word of God proclaimed. Does it require sitting still for a long time? Being physically present? Or quiet? Do worshipers need to read or have a sizable vocabulary? Who might be excluded? Pray like the prophets: *It doesn't have to be this way.* Then listen.

5. Name one or two books from this chapter that intrigue you. Support your pastor by reading them together. Partner up, laity and clergy.

Chapter Sixteen

A Benediction:
Blessing Your Work and Sending You Out

As you finish these chapters, my hopes for you are bold. Even urgent.

- **I hope you will remember that you are not miniatures of anything.**
  The Church's mission can't be *shrunk*. Our work doesn't come in a *fun size*. You don't celebrate with *dialed-down* worship. Or offer *scaled-down* ministries. You have a distinctive set of gifts that don't work in big settings. With them, you seek the kingdom *fully*. You offer yourselves *extravagantly*. You worship *lavishly*. You minister *wholly*. And God shows up. Not once your dashboard of attendance becomes compelling to the district office. Not when the praise band arrives. But now. *Really*.

- **I hope you will find seventy more strengths of small congregations.**
  The strengths in this book aren't designed as "fixes" for small congregations. And they certainly aren't a finished set. There are more. Perhaps many more. This book is an ongoing

invitation. *Reimagine your worship. Work differently. Look for more tools. And trust that you will find them.* God knows how to transform ordinary offerings into feasts with leftovers.

- **I hope you will experiment, flail, innovate, fail, diagnose, adapt, learn, and share.** Worship work and ministry have always required risk. And mess. There is no single optimal plan for success. There is no tidy one-size-fits-most program. The Incarnation just keeps nudging us to take the holy plunge into context and collaboration. *Help build the kingdom. Right here. With these people.* Along the way, you can expect to flounder, make do, goof up, and try again. And again. Like those who shared their stories for this book, you may be fearful of taking this plunge. But you also know what God says to fearful folks.

- **I hope you will lead the whole Church in exploring worship as participation.** Participation is your superpower. But participation is not simply a practical tool for forming people. It's also an essential theological commitment. Christian worship seeks nothing less than "full, conscious, and active participation." Clergy and laity. Engaging the work together. In an often-unpredictable exchange between God and the gathered. Small congregations can turn worship watchers into worship collaborators. You can invite all hands to touch, each voice to speak, and every body to co-create an offering to God. So quit playing by the limitations of big settings. *Lead on.*

- **I hope you recognize the stakes of your work. They are not just "for now." They are for the kingdom-to-come.**
  Divine love continually extends its reach. But the kingdom doesn't simply leap from one fully-formed success to the next. Instead, it starts small. It grows like an easily-overlooked mustard seed. This suggests that what the Church may need for the next 500 years is probably small now. And that we need faithful folks to work in easily-overlooked ways. In margins and edges. With inefficient explorations and uncertain results. In unexpected places and among unlikely people. Because this work is not just "for now." For the sake of *your* small congregation. This work is for the future—for the kingdom-to-come. For the sake of *all* congregations. And for the mission of divine love to all creation.

For the love of God, I hope you take up this work together.

Thanks for your ministry,

Teresa J. Stewart
Teresa@SmallChurch.org

PART 3

WORSHIP WONDERS
FOR SMALL GROUP STUDY

Three Unexpected Conversations for Small Congregations to Lead

Chapter Seventeen:
The Glorious Gospel of Making Do
Unleashing Unlikely Creativity

Chapter Eighteen:
Worship as an Alternate Possibility
Practicing the Kingdom

Chapter 19:
Holy Resistance
The Superpower of Outsiders, Underdogs, and Small Congregations

Ready for more?

- In addition to *worship strengths*, small congregations may also have distinctive *theological insights*.

- This bonus section invites you to start whole-congregation conversations around three insights. Each fits your gifts. Each requires your small-setting perspective. And each serves the mission of the whole Church.

- Invite your Sunday School classes and small groups to read each insight and start a conversation with the questions that follow.

- The insights are deeply rooted in the Christian tradition. But the Church needs you to explore them together. Then lead them for everyone.

Bonus Chapter Seventeen

The Glorious Gospel of Making Do
Unleashing Unlikely Creativity

Maybe you've heard it said that small congregations don't have enough to really flourish. At best, they can make do and maybe get by.

But what if making do is a holy practice— one revealed by God? And what if this practice is essential to recognizing the good news and its abundance for all creation?

It's an essential, hiding-in-plain-sight theme in the Bible: making do. God's work never depends on ideal plans, perfect people, or the right resources. Instead, with the boldness of divine love, God works with whatever and whoever. God makes do.

Surrounded by chaos and with no engineering blueprints, God created anyway. When God sought out a people to carry out the divine rescue plan, a nomad and his barren wife were a good enough start.

Remember when the plan called for a savior? No baby bed? A manger made do. No public relations team? Try some shepherds. Need credible witnesses? Grab some uneducated fishermen. Add in poor widows, tax collectors, and a sister who neglects her chores. Need more followers? Look for ordinary, hungry folks.

The make-do pattern continued with the Early Church. Need to build upon a rock? Try that bumbling denier named Peter. No cathedrals? Start in the catacombs. No articles of incorporation or tidy bylaws? No worries. We'll work it out in every language, place, and community. Not with ideal, perfect, and "right" resources. But with messy, here, and adaptable ones. Whatever and whoever. Perhaps because God is the never-give-up source of all those whatevers and whoevers to begin with. Scripture is pretty clear on this point. Making do is the preferred method of Incarnation. God comes for us just as we are. God works with what we have. And this method manages to unleash the good news. Surprisingly and powerfully. When divine love makes do, somehow there is more than enough for all.

But this connection between making do and enoughness isn't relegated to the Bible. It pours out into all of life. Made in the image of God, perhaps we shouldn't be surprised that humans work this way. And we shouldn't be surprised that social scientists have picked up on this pattern.

There's been a recent flurry of study on the subject of "making do." Researchers have studied stress in relation to creativity and productivity. They've examined how humans innovate and flourish even when conditions and resources are less than ideal. And while the work has been targeted toward businesses, organizations, and leaders, the practical lessons spill out beyond the intended audience.

Researchers have reminded us, for example, that the best solutions begin with identifying strengths rather than simply trying to list and fix weaknesses. Building on what you do well beats playing whack-a-mole with the stuff you don't. They've also reminded us that innovation is usually increased by including an outsider's perspective: a new way of seeing things. "Edge thinking" is powerful and necessary.

Finally, researchers have offered this gem of a lesson (drumroll, please): *the condition of having less actually unleashes greater imagination and possibilities.*

Stop a moment and reread that last sentence. It's stuffed full of hopeful paradox.

Scott Sonenshein makes the case in his recent book *Stretch*.[48] He's a professor of management who observes two critical mindsets: *chasing* and *stretching*. Chasing is that mindset of securing the best possible resources, the right skills, people, and tools. It assumes that there is one excellent model and one necessary toolbox. So the work requires procuring specific ideal tools to create a specific ideal thing.

But this mindset comes with a price. It overlooks what is already at hand and how it might be used *differently*. It ignores the peculiar power of making do. Sonenshein describes the trap of chasing: "It's difficult to be productive with what's already in hand when we're distracted by always looking for something in other people's hands." Chasing keeps us feeling like there's not enough, which is "harmful, upends success, and makes people miserable."[49]

---

[48] Scott Sonenshein, *Stretch: Unlock the Power of Less and Achieve More Than You Ever Imagined* (New York: HarperCollins, 2017).

[49] Sonenshein, *Stretch.*

Amen?

Stretching, on the other hand, works differently. The stretchy mindset ignores the possibility of a perfect toolbox. It starts with what is already in hand. How could it be used differently? What else around us is available? How does our resourcefulness and imagination point to another way? *No hammer in the toolbox? Use a brick. Or a hymnal. No inside experts? Look for outsiders with new experiences. Missing ingredients? Start a new recipe.* Stretch and make do.

Stretching unlocks new strengths. It sheds constraints. It improvises. Stretching finds treasure among trash. It embraces outsiders. Unleashes imagination. And reveals that sense of more-than-enoughness.

There is a power to having less. In both innovation and productivity.

Sonenshein unpacks these lessons in countless examples from business, education, sports, medicine, and history. And while he's not specifically talking to small congregations, the lessons should feel familiar. It's the *MacGyver* principle from the 1980s television show. No airplane? Start with a tent, wheelbarrow, lawnmower engine, and duct tape. Always duct tape.

More importantly, it's a *faith* principle. It's a holy way of operating that's been woven into us. God came for us ready to make do. So we come for the world. Just as it is. With whatever and whoever. And with the boldness of divine love and a wink of the Spirit, we know there is more than enough.

Start the Conversation

1. Share a story of when you had to make do. What did you notice?

2. Find examples of Bible stories without ideal plans, perfect people, or the "right" resources. What happened? Is it an example of *stretching* (making do) or *chasing?*

3. Does your congregation see itself as not being enough and having too little? Where do you notice this?

4. Does your congregation quietly chase one excellent model of worship and one excellent toolbox? Where or how do you notice the chase?

5. Now prayerfully brainstorm together. What are you overlooking? In your congregation? Your neighborhood? Your community? Your region? How could you improvise toward the kingdom of God with the abundance of what is already among you? Be specific. Write it down. And keep adding to it.

Chapter Eighteen

Worship as Alternate Possibility

Practicing the Kingdom

Maybe you've heard it said that the effectiveness of small congregations is unlikely and weak.

But what if the kingdom of God has a habit of showing up among unlikely places and weak people ready for another possibility?

It does. And practicing this habit is called worship.

It's a blockbuster, game-changing Bible story: the Hebrews liberated from the death-dealing power of Pharaoh. Think back on it. Recall the years of suffering. The reluctance of Moses. The underhanded negotiation of Pharaoh. The escalating plagues. And the final epic escape.

Then ask yourself this question: When *exactly* were the Hebrew children freed? Was it with the persuasion of locusts? Or during the Passover preparations? Or with the parting of the Red Sea?

Renown theologian Walter Brueggemann says the answer is none of the above. Instead, he suggests that the liberation occurred in that unlikely encounter with a burning bush.[50] When Moses met up with the One who heard the cries of hurting people and would not turn away. In that moment, Moses experienced a not-business-as-usual vision. He saw an "alternate possibility." A way previously unimaginable. And this new way changed everything. The encounter overturned expectations. It rewrote reality. These were not enslaved "nobodies." They were precious, priceless children of God! There was an alternate possibility: a God who listened, loved, acted, and persisted on their behalf!

It doesn't have to be this way!

This new reality would require more struggles, bricks, and long years to work out the details. But everything had already changed. Irreversibly. Because they glimpsed a different possibility. Because they saw a new reality. Because they had a new destination. And knowing this destination, they would never be enslaved again. They were freed—*already*. They simply had to practice this "already" into its full reality.[51]

There is another way!

Glimpses of alternate possibilities are powerful that way. Entirely unlikely. Wholly transforming.

Just look at the work of Jesus. It's drenched in that combination of "unlikely" and "transforming." That's because Jesus shows us the fullest picture of God's alternate possibility for creation. The divine "other way" is packed into Jesus's birth, life, teaching, ministry, death, and resurrection. And Jesus gives us a shorthand

---

[50] I was reawakened to this story by Bishop Michael Curry, *Love Is the Way: Holding on to Hope in Troubling Times* (New York: Avery, 2020).

[51] Fancy word: prolepsis (anticipating a future that is lived out now).

term for this alternate possibility: *the kingdom of God*. It's the new reality where children matter, the weak are made strong, the hungry are fed, the lost are found, the hurt are healed, injustices are overturned, and death is not the final word.

And here's the really important part. Christians are expected to catch a glimpse of this kingdom's not-business-as-usual vision. Then we're expected to practice it into full reality. Like those already-liberated, precious, priceless Hebrew children once Moses set foot on holy ground. We can see this divine, new reality and set our destination: *Earth as it is in heaven.* Many steps must follow. But we know where we are going.

Pause here to take in that wild paradox. It's a curious feature of the kingdom of God (and other alternative possibilities). We can glimpse it around us. It's here. *Now. Already.* Remember Jesus's assurance that the kingdom is already among us? But it's also not fully here. *Not yet.* There are still folks left out. There is still work to be done. That's why we recognize Christ's presence in the bread and wine of communion. Here and now. We can taste the new reality! But we also look forward to the time when Christ comes in final victory. We anticipate the fine, full feast yet to come. When the transformation is complete. The kingdom of God is somehow *both.* Now. And not yet.

Our heads may be spinning by now. Alternate possibilities. The kingdom of God. Now. And not yet. What in the world does this have to do with small-congregation worship?

Everything, it turns out. So hang on.

Worship is nothing less than practicing-into-being the

kingdom of God. In worship, we enact the kingdom like a full-body contact sport. We don't just *think* about it. It's not a between-the-ears-only event. We rehearse its alternate possibility with our bodies. We run its plays. We practice its scales. We hit its marks. We take on those kingdom patterns of welcoming, giving, receiving, forgiving, blessing, feeding, and belonging.

By so doing, we glimpse again that divine, unlikely transforming destination: the kingdom. *It's here among us!* And we create muscle memory for the work ahead. Our bodies remember the patterns: *There is another way.* Worship takes the alternative possibility—God's reality—and makes it our reality. *Earth as it is in heaven.* Worship is not passive or performance. It is active kingdom practice. The here-and-now rehearsal. For the yet-to-come salvation of all creation.

And with weekly rehearsal, worship becomes a compass. It orients us toward our destination. It works like a carpenter hanging a plumb line. It marks what is true so that our work is sound. And, of course, worship still functions like stumbling upon a burning-but-not-consumed bush. It defies the usual rules of the world. And somehow both reveals and creates another way.

So that's your job for worship. Help reveal and create the kingdom of God among you. Bring the not-yet into the now. Point to the destination. Where there are no "nobodies," only priceless, precious children. Seek out folks longing for an alternate possibility. Include them as full participants. Stand for them and with them. Then enact these not-business-as-usual patterns together: welcome, give, receive, forgive, bless, feed, belong. Your worship should be a kingdom encounter where children matter, the weak are made strong, the hungry are fed, the lost are found, the hurt are healed, injustices are overturned, and death is not the final word by a long shot.

Need some examples for inspiration?

One small congregation invites folks from its homeless ministry to read or act out the scripture each week. Their voices and bodies lead the congregation. They are treated as givers and not merely receivers. And sometimes they offer surprising alternate-possibility insights: *The woman playing the Good Samaritan paused to weep and cradle the man beaten by robbers. It felt like we heard the scripture for the first time.* Persons viewed as worthless to the world are precious, priceless, and qualified for kingdom work. So worship makes that clear. *The kingdom is already among us.*

Another small congregation focuses on children. They invite children to help serve communion, tend the baptismal font, and remind worshipers to splash in joy each week. The pastor finds creative ways to include children's outside-of-church talents. They sing, play instruments, dance, and act in worship. And it's not just the children of members. Or those who can sit still and use good manners. It's *all* children. As one member described it, the congregation decided to trade in tidiness for a taste of the kingdom.

Now. Already.

Another set of small congregations share a building. There was weekly worship in English and Spanish but little interaction between the groups. So they changed their worship times to include a shared monthly meal between the services. It's awkward sometimes. But they're learning that communion goes well with both green bean casserole and tamales. Some worshipers say they can better imagine that final victory feast when Jesus returns. Because they've already smelled what's cooking.

There's more to come.

Maybe "fixing" your worship is not about getting the best sound system, hiring the right experts, or polishing the production value. Maybe it's about starting with the divine alternate possibility. *It doesn't have to be this way.* Then imagining the previously unimaginable—for your community and all creation. *There is another way.* And finally practicing it until the kingdom spills out of your sanctuary doors and creates the new reality. Entirely. Wholly. The unlikely transformation . . . *Earth as it is in heaven, indeed!*

Ready to worship?

Start the Conversation

1. Share a story of when you've encountered an alternate possibility that changed you—even though there were still struggles and long years ahead.

2. Spend time together looking through the gospels for the kingdom of God or the kingdom of heaven. What do you notice? What are its characteristics? Who participates?

3. Where do these characteristics and participants show up in your worship? How do you practice God's alternate possibility together?

4. When have you experienced the kingdom of God? Share the story in lavish detail.

5. How could you more fully practice and re-create the kingdom of God in your worship? Don't be afraid to start small. God isn't. Who and what needs to be included?

Chapter Nineteen

Holy Resistance

The Superpower of Outsiders, Underdogs, and Small Congregations

Maybe you've heard it said that the resistance of small congregations is an exasperating, ineffective, and self-defeating form of power.

But what if resistance is also a holy kind of leadership revealed by God and essential to the whole Church?

It is.

"They may die, but you can't kill them." The district superintendent was describing a curious trait of small congregations: resistance.

Resistance is the quiet superpower of small groups, outsiders, and underdogs. It's their muscular ability to push against a dominant force with unconventional tactics. Like slow-walking the authorized plan, losing the paperwork, or subtly changing the official story. Resistance cleverly avoids complying with orders and outcomes that it disagrees with. Even if there is no appeals process. Faced with established power, resistance quietly plants its feet and insists: *No. There is another way. We won't give in to those plans. Just wait and see.*

And resistance is nothing to be trifled with. Just ask the parent of a teen. Or a well-armed colonial regime that can't seem to take control. Or your denominational headquarters in the process of rolling out the latest congregational success initiative. Resistance is a peculiar kind of power. Unpredictable. Slippery. And countering it can feel like nailing Jello to a wall. Just ask that district superintendent.

Here's why. Resistance refuses to play by the usual rules. Instead, it wiggles between them and reinterprets them. It replaces direct force with creativity and persistence. It brushes aside convention, convenience, and practicality. And this is the really crucial move: *resistance locks onto a vision of change.* Resistance always has a goal of what could be. A later curfew. Local, nonviolent governance. Less paperwork and control by headquarters.

This vision of *what-could-be* then fuels resistance to push against *whatever-is* with *whatever-it-has.* Even when it has very little. Even when pushing is risky. Or even when the goal appears not merely unlikely but impossible. And this makes resistance formidable. Because the goal of resistance is not trying to win the game. *Instead, resistance ultimately seeks to change the game.*

That's why it's a favorite tool of justice movements and the preferred fuel of "alternate possibilities." Small groups, outsiders, and underdogs can take on powerful, oppressive systems. With little more than an unlikely vision and the willingness of folks to sit at lunch counters, march across bridges, or wear handcuffs.

Bottom line: resistance has a reputation for being a mere irritant. But it can be immensely powerful. Endlessly adaptive. Exasperatingly stubborn. Game-changing.

And there's another overlooked truth about resistance. It's essential to our faith. That's right—*absolutely essential*. Resistance shows up in every book of the Bible. In fact, the salvation story can't be told without it. The good news depends on it!

Skeptical? Start with our first glimpse of God.

Genesis doesn't begin with creation. It begins with resistance. Before shaping fins, feathers, and folks, God first pushes back against the destructive watery chaos. God defies the established order of the cosmos and crafts a protective dome. For the Hebrew worldview, the picture of this defiance is surprising and tender. God stretches across the deep as a shield—to make a safe place for life to flourish. In the beginning, God refuses to play by the usual rules. God imagines an impossible *what-could-be*. God, the Creator, resists to make it so.

But resistance doesn't end there. The divine rescue plan continues with resistance. God chooses small groups, outsiders, and underdogs to make a new way with unconventional tactics. Together, they raise valleys and lower mountains. Without official building permits or commercial-grade earth-moving equipment. They defy expectations and reimagine *what-could-be* with the Spirit and whatever-they-have. Which often is not much. But also enough.

Remember Moses leading a bunch of enslaved "nobodies" and weaponizing frogs? Remember the winking defiance of Shiprah and Puah to protect babies from Pharaoh's kill order? Remember Nathan confronting the corrupt power of King David with nothing more than a "gotcha" story? Or remember

179

the pregnancy of an unwed teenage girl named Mary subverting the Roman Empire?

In fact, Mary offers the perfect theme song for all this biblical resisting. Remember the resistance from Luke 2? Reread the Magnificat. It upends the usual rules of power in favor of weary, forgotten, oppressed, hopeless, and hungry folks. And take special note: The tune is not a lament. It's filled with joy and enthusiasm. Even when things are difficult. As if the biblical *what-could-be* we seek is a magnificent, good hope. An entirely new game where all creation wins. Because it does. Just wait and see.

And then, of course, there's Jesus. The Great Resistor. He pushes back against official power with a ministry brimming with Sabbath-healing, beggar-recognizing, leper-touching, temple-tossing, widow-noticing, meal-multiplying, scarcity-subverting, and child-welcoming. You could probably name a few more. But this much is clear: Jesus, the Word of God, writes our salvation with resistance.

Our scriptures themselves are works of resistance. They push back against the world around them. They reimagine the expected orders and outcomes. They rewrite the game. For example, the Hebrew Bible (or Old Testament) pokes at the dominant Babylonian view that a warrior god created the world in an act of violence: *No. God is good and blesses creation.* The New Testament defies Rome's ultimate power grab: *No. Caesar's word is not final. God can overturn even a death sentence on a cross.*

But what does any of this have to do with small congregations?

This is where things get exciting. Because you already know how to do resistance. You are uniquely positioned to be experts in this superpower. You have the distinctive insight of small groups, outsiders, and underdogs. You know how to stretch, make do, and adapt. Don't let anyone convince you these are not powerful strengths!

But the strength of your resistance was never meant to be aimed at things like moving your denominational leadership toward early retirement. It's meant for bigger stuff. You are called to a higher purpose: *Holy Resistance*. You are called to be leaders in this faithful response on behalf of the whole Church.

So, what in the world is Holy Resistance?

It's the goal of Holy Resistance that distinguishes it. And the goal is pretty simple. Holy Resistance seeks the kingdom of God. Right here on Earth. In each community. *Your* community. And it's not afraid to push back against barriers with unconventional tactics. It's not afraid to change the game. Scripture announces the new rules. Holy Resistance makes a shield for life to flourish. Even against overwhelming forces. Holy Resistance speaks truth to power on behalf of the powerless. Even when it's risky or dangerous. Holy Resistance stands on the side of the weary, forgotten, oppressed, hopeless, and hungry. Joyfully! Expectantly! Even when it looks like there's not enough for everyone.

Sound like an overwhelming job? Don't worry. Holy Resistance is never a DIY task. The Spirit guides, encourages, and even helps with the heavy lifting. Remember that the rollout of the good news didn't start with a grandly scaled campaign. It started in the backwater of Bethlehem. With a bunch of fieldhands, not a public relations firm. It continued with disciples that were more bumble than polish. You're qualified to do this work. And you are not alone.

But maybe you need some inspiration to get started.

For one congregation, Holy Resistance meant starting an after-school program so children had a safe place to go. Even though the church budget said it was impossible. Even though their building made it impractical. And even though others in the community claimed after-school childcare wasn't a problem. They prayed, saved, scavenged, and recruited carpenters and helpers. They begged, prayed some more. And did it anyway. The children came and flourished.

For another church, Holy Resistance meant welcoming addicts and alcoholics who needed a meeting place for their support group. Even though it was an unconventional ministry for the area. Even though some neighbors (and lifelong members) did not want "those kinds" of people around. And even though there were questions about how it might affect maintenance, insurance, and (gasp) tithing members. So they prayed, had tough conversations, shared personal stories, listened. And added a potluck to make the meeting night more inviting for all the people anyway. It felt joyful!

For another church, Holy Resistance meant making last-minute birthday cakes for the local domestic violence shelter. For children who would otherwise have no celebration. Even though these children would likely just move away in a few weeks. Even though the need was unpredictable to coordinate and seemed so minor compared to the practical needs of these families. So they prayed while they baked, made a list of cooks on call, and treated it like a big deal anyway. They were right. It was a big, game-changing deal. One child at a time.

For yet another congregation, Holy Resistance meant providing relief and advocacy for transient farm workers and their families. Even though the families would not stick around and become members. Even though the needs were often overwhelming and unexpected. And even though some of the advocates risked arrest by confronting the justice system. They prayed, started new relationships, changed, allowed their hearts to break, and did it anyway. And somehow, in the process, they saw the kingdom among them.

So where should you start your Holy Resistance?

First, start praying this way. Get out of your sanctuary. Leave your building. Walk or drive your community. All the streets. See all the people. Especially the ones no one else sees. Look with the eyes of Jesus the Great Resistor. And repeat: *Lord, may your kingdom come. Right here. Like heaven. We know the risk. And we are ready anyway. With all we have and all You are.*

Then remember: God has already uniquely equipped you for this work. The larger Church has been good at dismissing the power of resistance with an eye roll. But you can summon Holy Resistance *faith-fully.* You understand perspectives of small groups, outsiders, and underdogs. You know out-of-the-way, overlooked, powerless places and people. You don't have to wait for a grand denominational initiative. Use your superpower right where you are! You see the needs. And, most importantly, you have felt the divine love that resists *with* you, reaches across the chaos and whispers: *No. There is another way. Earth as it is in heaven. Just wait and see.*

Alleluiah! And amen!

Start the Conversation

1. Share a story about when you've noticed heels-dug-in resistance in your congregation or community. Does it make you smile or feel exasperated?

2. Brainstorm together. What unconventional tactics might small groups, outsiders, and underdogs use against official power? List at least ten.

3. Prophets in the Bible are professional-grade resistors. Name your favorite prophet and describe how they wield the power of resistance.

4. When have you witnessed or experienced Holy Resistance? How would you describe Holy Resistance to a neighbor? What makes it different from other kinds of resistance?

5. Set aside what is conventional, practical, or likely. Start to imagine where the kingdom of God might break into your community. What is one step of Holy Resistance that you could take to welcome it?

Printed in Great Britain
by Amazon

45236280R00111